W9-BXE-209

—Diseases and People—

ASTHMA

Alvin and Virginia Silverstein
and Laura Silverstein Nunn

Enslow Publishers, Inc.

44 Fadem Road   PO Box 38
Box 699   Aldershot
Springfield, NJ 07081 Hants GU12 6BP
USA   UK

For our dear friend Dorothy Williams,
in memory of her daughter,
Darlene Williams Cole

Library of Congress Cataloging-in-Publication Data

Silverstein, Alvin.
    Asthma / Alvin and Virginia Silverstein and Laura Silverstein Nunn.
        p. cm. — (Diseases and people)
    Includes bibliographical references and index.
    ISBN 0-89490-712-3
    1. Asthma—Juvenile literature. I. Silverstein, Virginia B.
II. Nunn, Laura Silverstein. III. Title. IV. Series.
RC591.S55 1997
616.2'38—dc20   96-29095
                                          CIP

Printed in the United States of America

10 9 8 7 6 5 4 3 2 1

Illustration Credits: The Bettmann Archive, p. 6; BottomLine Marketing, pp. 83, 88; Courtesy of National Library of Medicine, pp. 13, 15, 36, 94; Courtesy of NIAID, NIH, pp. 10, 53, 55, 57; Courtesy of Thomas F. Plaut, M.D., Asthma Consultants, p. 59; DeVilbiss Health Care, Inc., p. 67; Globe Photos, Inc., p. 46; National Heart, Lung, and Blood Institute, p. 29; National Institutes of Health, p. 41; Reuters/Bettmann, p. 23; S.C. Delaney/United States EPA, pp. 86, 97; United States Department of Agriculture, p. 33.

Cover Illustration: Mrs. Kevin Scheibel

Contents

Acknowledgment

The authors owe warm thanks to Dr. Arthur J. Torre for his careful reading of the manuscript and for the wealth of information and insights that he provided. He helped to put everything into perspective.

ASTHMA

What is it? A chronic lung disorder in which the airways are inflamed and hyperreactive; they narrow in response to specific "triggers," making breathing difficult.

Who gets it? Asthma can affect all nationalities, races, and ethnic groups. It frequently appears in young children. Before puberty, it occurs more often in boys, but among adults, the sexes as equally represented.

How do you get it? By inheriting an undetermined number of genes that make the airways hyperreactive and increase susceptibility to allergies. Asthma episodes may be triggered by air pollution (including cigarette smoke), plant pollens, animal dander, dust mites, and molds, as well as cold air and exercise. Asthma is not contagious and is not spread by germs, although an infectious disease may trigger episodes.

What are the symptoms? Coughing, wheezing, a feeling of tightness in the chest, shortness of breath, and sucking in of the chest skin during episodes. Episodes often occur during the night.

How is it treated? Self-management with hand-held inhalers containing corticosteroids or other anti-inflammatory drugs normally keeps asthma under control; bronchodilators are used to stop episodes or prevent exercise-induced asthma. Immunotherapy by injections of small amounts of allergens can desensitize asthma patients to these allergens. Exercise and avoidance of known triggers are also important in asthma management.

How can it be prevented? Avoidance of asthma triggers can prevent most episodes; air conditioners and air filters can reduce the effects of air pollution.

Although medical treatment for asthma was very limited at that time, Theodore Roosevelt was able to manage his asthma and live a very productive life.

1

Breath of Life

Theodore Roosevelt was a remarkable man. He was a hunter, a soldier, a conservationist, and president of the United States. Yet during his childhood, no one suspected Teddy Roosevelt would lead such an active life. He was a sickly child, in and out of hospitals because of his severe asthma episodes. He was often bedridden with a severe chronic cough. People did not think the frail child would live into adulthood. Yet Teddy was a strong and determined individual. Medical treatment for asthma was very limited at that time, so Roosevelt tried some treatments of his own. He did strenuous exercises daily and managed to improve his lung capacity, which decreased the frequency and severity of his episodes. Although Teddy Roosevelt could not eliminate his asthma, he made it so manageable that he was able to live a very productive life.[1]

Teddy Roosevelt learned to value every breath he took since breathing was not easy for him at times. Most people take breathing for granted. We do not usually spend our days thinking about our next breath. In fact, breathing is automatic; it just happens without our consciously thinking about it or even realizing we are doing it. Breathing does not become noticeable unless we are running to catch a bus or gasping in a room filled with cigarette smoke. People with asthma, however, *do* think about breathing—every single day.

Asthma is one of our most common chronic illnesses, yet most people are not sure what it is. Asthma is a lung disorder in which the airways, the muscular tubes through which air flows into and out of the lungs, are inflamed and hyperreactive—inhaled irritants cause the airway walls to contract, blocking the airflow. As the airways become narrow, less oxygen is able to pass into and out of the lungs in each breath. Breathing becomes difficult, with episodes of wheezing, coughing, and a feeling of tightness in the chest.

Asthma can affect anyone, but it most commonly occurs among children. Asthma is responsible for more absences from school and work than any other chronic illness, costing society billions of dollars each year.

People with asthma are born with a tendency to have hyperreactive airways. That is, their breathing passages overreact to things in the environment that do not affect most people. When a person with asthma inhales foreign particles in the air—such as house dust, molds, plant pollens, or air pollution—the muscles in the walls of the breathing passages contract, and the lining of the airways swells and produces extra mucus, adding to the breathing difficulties. Allergies play a key role in asthma. Skin tests can be done to identify the allergens that may be triggering an asthma episode or causing chronic inflammation. Exercise, cold air, and emotional stress can also be asthma triggers.

People can die from asthma. Fortunately, this is not common; and, sadly, the deaths that do occur are unnecessary. Some people who have asthma are misdiagnosed. If the condition goes untreated, it will worsen. When an asthma episode occurs, immediate treatment is essential to prevent it from escalating. Asthma symptoms can be relieved by using drugs called bronchodilators, which will quickly open up the airways. Anti-inflammatory drugs, taken regularly, can help keep asthma under control and reduce or even eliminate the need for bronchodilators. (Reliance on bronchodilators alone, without treating the chronic inflammation, can contribute to asthma death.)

Air pollution has become a major problem for people with asthma. Trying to avoid pollutants is practically impossible, which may make asthmatics feel like they cannot even walk out of their houses. Federal and state environmental agencies are continually fighting for stricter regulations to reduce sources of air pollutants.

Although emergency medical treatment may sometimes be necessary to relieve a severe episode, asthma patients rely

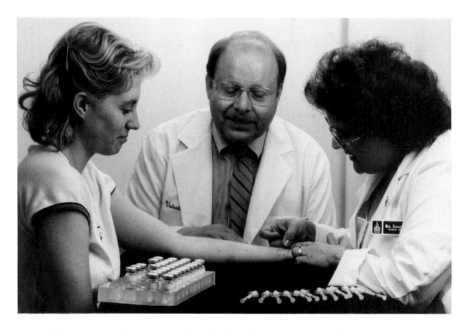

Skin tests can be done to identify the allergens that may be triggering an asthma episode.

mainly on self-management to control their condition. Education plays a major role in self-management. When asthma patients learn as much as they can about their condition, they are better equipped to handle difficult situations and are able to treat their asthma accordingly.

Although treatments now available can keep asthma under control, so that a person with this chronic condition can lead a normal life, there is presently no cure. However, researchers are certain that asthma is caused by genetic factors. Scientists continue to look for a gene or genes that are responsible for the development of hyperreactive airways in susceptible people. This discovery could one day lead to a cure.

2

Asthma in History

Asthma was first described thousands of years ago by Hippocrates, the Greek physician known as "the father of medicine." The name for this condition comes from the Greek word *asthma,* which means "panting." Hippocrates used this term to describe the wheezing sound that asthma patients make, which is the most recognizable symptom of the disease.[1]

In A.D. 200, another Greek physician, Galen, became the first person to document the clinical signs of asthma. He observed that difficulty in breathing occurred after strenuous exercise or any other type of work and caused flushed cheeks and bulging eyes, as if the person was being strangled.[2] Galen also observed the overproduction of mucus in asthma: "If the breath makes a raucous sound, this indicates obstruction due

Galen, a Greek physician, was the first person to document the clinical signs of asthma.

to an abundance of viscous or thick humors which are stuck to the bronchi of the lung and cannot be easily loosed."[3]

One of the earliest attempts to treat asthma was made in the A.D. 600s by Paulus Aegineta. He concentrated on trying to rid patients of the excessive musus by giving them specific medicines that would break up the mucus plugs and liquify the mucus so it could easily be coughed up.

Five centuries later, Maimonides, a famous Jewish physician and philosopher, made an interesting discovery. He suggested that heredity may be responsible for the occurrence of asthma after he noticed that the condition appeared to run in families. He also described some typical triggers of asthma and advised his patients to avoid apricots, black beans, cauliflower, garlic, lettuce, peaches, pumpkin, turnip, and watermelon. His remedies for asthma episodes included chicken soup, freshwater fish, mint, parsley, and radishes.[4]

A sixteenth-century physician named Jerome Cardan treated King Edward VI of England after the king suffered an asthma episode. Dr. Cardan became the first to suggest that asthma was caused by environmental factors. The king appeared to be cured once the doctor removed the feather pillows from his bed. This was the first connection between asthma and allergies.

In 1698, a physician, Sir John Floyer, claimed that asthma was due to a "contracture of the muscular fibers of the bronchi." This was the first medical description of the underlying cause of asthma.[5] He also was one of the first to

Jerome Cardan, a sixteenth century physician, was the first to suggest that asthma was caused by environmental factors.

acknowledge that asthma can lead to death after he reported the death of an eighteen-month-old infant due to asthma.

In 1794, Dr. William Cullen from Edinburgh, Scotland, called attention to the difficulty in diagnosing asthma. Since the symptoms of asthma appeared to be similar to other respiratory illnesses, he complained that:

> The term asthma has been commonly applied by the vulgar, and even by many . . . (specialists), to every case of difficult breathing [dyspnea]. . . . By not distinguishing it with sufficient accuracy from other cases of Dyspnea, they have introduced a great deal of confusion into their treatises on this subject.[6]

Aerosols for treating asthma were finally invented in the 1800s, and a variety of medications were available by prescription. Some of these medications included potassium iodide and the extract from the root of the Brazilian ipecacuanha plant. (The active ingredient, ipecac, is used today to induce vomiting to treat poisoning. It was dropped as an asthma therapy after it was noticed that druggists who ground the ipecacuanha roots developed occupational asthma!) Some of the bronchodilators included coffee and atropine. Atropine cigarettes were introduced in the early 1900s; one popular brand was named Asmadore. Other bronchodilators that began to be used in the 1900s were ephedrine and theophylline.[7]

An Old Disease Gained New Recognition

Although asthma has been around for many years, it was not until the 1940s that allergic diseases were finally becoming recognized as a health hazard that affected millions. People with asthma felt helpless against this disease, since little was known about it and there were very few organizations that concentrated on asthma treatment.

A New "Home" Helped Children in Need

In the early 1920s, Fannie E. Lorber founded the Denver Sheltering Home, which later expanded and became known as the National Home for Jewish Children. This home started as a day-care center for children. It housed children who had parents with serious illnesses, such as tuberculosis, and also children themselves who had tuberculosis. By the end of the 1930s, though, advances in tuberculosis treatment meant that there was less need for "the Home" anymore. The Home then began to focus on another devastating lung disease—asthma.

The managers of the Home decided in 1939 to start a program dedicated to children whose asthma appeared hopeless and unmanageable. They felt this program would be very beneficial, especially after they took in two orphan children with severe asthma and the children's symptoms disappeared under their care.

Could the Parents Be to Blame?

Looking for someone to head up the program for asthmatic children, the National Home for Jewish Children hired Dr. C. Murray Peshkin, an allergy specialist from Mount Sinai Hospital in New York City. At Mount Sinai, Dr. Peshkin had made some of his own observations about asthma. He noticed that in many cases, children with severe asthma showed immediate improvement when they were taken away from

17

their home environment. He came to the conclusion that perhaps the parents were the cause of their asthma. He viewed the disease as an emotional reaction to stress in the family. At the Home, Dr. Peshkin emphasized a treatment approach that he called parentectomy—taking the child away from the family as a way of treating severe asthma.[8] Since little was known about the causes of asthma at that time, his theory seemed reasonable. Dr. Peshkin believed that an eighteen- to twenty-four-month separation was necessary for a lasting cure. A two-year stay at the Home became the standard practice for asthma treatment for more than a decade. Although many experts did not agree with Dr. Peshkin, there were very few alternatives.

In 1951, the Home hired its first full-time medical director, Dr. Allan Hurst. He became the first person to openly question Dr. Peshkin's theories about parentectomy. Dr. Hurst started one of the earliest research efforts to prove that asthma was not just an emotional illness—but that important changes in the body were occurring during an asthma episode. These changes affected the immune system, which normally defends the body against disease germs. Dr. Hurst reported his research findings in a 1952 presentation to the American Medical Association.

Allergy Is the Key

In 1957, the Home set up a new asthma research facility called the Children's Asthma Research Institute and Hospital (CARIH). A year later, Dr. Samuel C. Bukantz was hired as its medical director. He launched a series of behavioral studies. The CARIH researchers found that some asthma patients were "rapid remitters," who quickly got well when they moved to the Home, away from their families. Other children, however, were "steroid dependent"—their asthma could not be controlled without drugs.[9]

Although Dr. Peshkin was fascinated with these new findings, he refused to abandon his theory of parentectomy. He still believed strongly that the key to asthma lay in psychoanalytic causes and treatment, while the director of the institute, Dr. Bukantz, believed there should be more balance between the medical and psychological approaches. This put a strain on their working relationship. Finally, Dr. Bukantz demanded that the board at CARIH make a choice between him and Dr. Peshkin. The decision was made—Dr. Bukantz stayed, and Dr. Peshkin left in 1962.

In 1966, a husband-and-wife immunology research team at CARIH, Kimishige and Teruko Ishizaka, made a major research breakthrough: the discovery of immunoglobulin E (IgE), known as the allergy antibody. They found that many people who had asthma had larger amounts of IgE in their blood that people without asthma. People with asthma were more sensitive to their environment than nonallergic people.

During the 1960s, Dr. Kenneth Purcell, the head of psychology at CARIH, finally put the myth of parentectomy to rest. He clarified that parents are not the cause of asthma episodes but play a rather important role in asthma treatment. It is necessary for the parents and children to educate themselves and work together in an effort to effectively manage the disease.[10]

The Discovery of "Twitchy Lungs"

In the 1960s, Dr. Irving Itkin reported the basic defect in asthma—the hyperreactive airways in the lungs, sometimes called "twitchy lungs." This was additional evidence that asthma was not the result of emotional stress. It was then observed, however, that although stress does not cause asthma, it can trigger asthma symptoms, but only in someone who already has "twitchy lungs."

By the 1970s, researchers discovered common triggers of asthma, such as allergens (plant pollens, animal danders, dusts, molds, and so forth), histamine, cold air, cigarette smoke, air pollution, exercise, and emotional reactions. Researchers also showed that not all asthma patients are allergic and not all allergic people have asthma. Allergy is just one of many triggers of asthma.

By the early 1990s, asthma specialists had become aware that airway inflammation plays a key role in the disease. Lack of awareness of this factor and inappropriate treatment were actually contributing to asthma deaths. Chronic inflammation, if untreated for five years, can lead to permanent damage to the airways. In 1991, the National Institutes of Health issued new guidelines for the diagnosis and treatment of asthma. The Global Strategy for Asthma Management and Prevention, issued in 1993 by a joint workshop conducted by representatives of the National Heart, Lung, and Blood Institute and the World Health Organization, emphasized the importance of this new focus.[11]

3

What Is Asthma?

Jackie Joyner-Kersee, a track and field star, showed a talent for sports from the time she was a little girl. At the age of ten, she even outran her brother Al, who later won an Olympic gold medal. In high school, Jackie starred in basketball and volleyball. It was not until college, however, that she really started to take athletics seriously. She dreamed of being in the Olympics and winning a gold medal. Jackie was such an extraordinary athlete that achieving her goal was definitely a possibility.

In college, Jackie was faced with something that put a snag in her plans. She started to experience a tightening in her chest and a shortness of breath. She noticed that her symptoms worsened when she exercised. When she told her coach, Bob Kersee (who eventually became her husband), he thought she was slacking off. Jackie's problem persisted, though, so she saw Dr. Roger Katz, a Los Angeles allergist, who believed she had asthma associated with exercise. However, Jackie informed Dr. Katz that her asthma was no longer occurring just after exercising, but all the time. She had developed a full-blown case of asthma.

At the same time Jackie became aware of her asthma, she noticed that she was having a reaction to certain foods like peanuts, pitted fruits, and fish. It became clear to Dr. Katz that her asthma was caused by her allergies.

After a complete analysis was made of Jackie's condition, she was able to receive the proper medication to control the asthma. The young athlete did not let asthma stand in the way of her dream of the Olympics. Jackie took medication before and after exercising to prevent asthma episodes. She also found that doing warm-ups was very helpful. In 1988, Jackie Joyner-Kersee achieved her goal: She made it to the Olympics and won several gold medals. In 1992, she did it again. She won another gold medal to add to her collection. In 1996, she won a bronze medal in her final Olympics, in Atlanta.

Jackie Joyner-Kersee turned her frightening illness into something she could live with. She refused to let asthma take over her life and take away her dreams.[1]

Asthma, also known as bronchial asthma, is a chronic lung disorder. It involves an inflammation of the bronchial tubes that causes the airways in the lungs to become narrow, making it very difficult to breathe. Although asthma is a lifelong disease, its effects are usually completely reversible. In other words, with the proper management and treatment, the

Jackie Joyner-Kersee does not let asthma stand in her way. By taking medication before and after exercising and by doing warm-ups she has been able to prevent asthma episodes.

symptoms can be either reduced or even eliminated. However, asthma cannot be cured. Although the symptoms may disappear for awhile, they can return at any time.

Who Has Asthma?

It is estimated that 12 to 15 million Americans suffer from asthma. Two to 5 million of them are children. This estimate may be conservative, considering that people with asthma are sometimes misdiagnosed or they may not know that they have this disease. People often dismiss their coughing or wheezing, thinking it is just a cold or being out of shape.

Asthma can affect anyone, all over the world. It does not discriminate. There is no place that is asthma-free. It occurs in all races. However, blacks have a much higher incidence of asthma than whites, and blacks are three times as likely as whites to die from asthma.

Asthma can occur at any age, but it most commonly occurs in children. Asthma is more easily detected in children because children's lungs are so much smaller than adults and they are more severely affected when their airways become blocked. Until puberty, boys are more likely than girls to develop asthma. After puberty, however, the sexes start to even out in numbers of asthma cases. Asthma is responsible for nearly five hundred thousand hospital admissions each year and causes more absences from school and work than any other chronic illness. This disease costs the United States more than $6 billion each year.

The incidence of asthma is on the rise. The number of asthma cases has doubled in the last twenty years. The number of asthma-related deaths recorded has increased to over five thousand per year, also doubling in the last two decades. This number may not be as large as the number of deaths from other diseases, but many doctors believe death from asthma is usually avoidable.

It is not quite clear why there has been an increase in asthma cases and deaths, but there are many theories. Some people point to the growth of cities and say that the added air pollution is wreaking havoc on the sensitive airways of asthma patients. Other people theorize that there may not be an actual increase in the number of deaths related to asthma but rather an improvement in diagnosis and reporting of the disease. In the past, doctors were more likely to misdiagnose people with asthma. Without proper treatment, their condition grew worse—and if they died because of their illness, no one knew that it was because of asthma.

What Causes Asthma?

Asthma is one of the least understood chronic diseases today. No one is quite sure what causes it. Through years of research, scientists have discovered a link between asthma and heredity. Researchers have yet to discover a specific asthma gene, but it has been found that those with asthma have inherited hyperreactive airways, or "twitchy lungs." Their lungs react and become irritated even by small amounts of things in the environment, such as dust or pollen, that do not bother most people at all.

Studies have shown that a close relative of someone with asthma (such as a brother or a sister or a child) is thirteen times more likely to develop asthma by age forty-nine, compared with a person with no family history of asthma, and thirty-three times more likely to develop it by age sixty-five.[2]

How Do Normal Lungs Function?

Before we can understand how asthma occurs, we need to explore how our lungs normally work. When we breathe in, or inhale, oxygen from the air enters the lungs and is absorbed into the bloodstream, which carries it to the many cells of the body. Meanwhile, carbon dioxide, a waste product of the cells, is carried by the blood to the lungs and is forced out of the body when we exhale. With each breath, about ten to fourteen times a minute, an adult takes in about 1 pint (0.5 liter) of air.

The respiratory system looks very much like an upside-down tree. When you breathe, air comes in through your mouth and nose, down your throat (the pharynx) and through your voice box (the larynx) and continues down the main breathing tube, called the windpipe or trachea. The air then goes through the two large bronchial tubes (bronchi), which lead into the right and left lungs. The bronchi branch into even smaller, almost threadlike tubes, called bronchioles. The bronchi and the larger bronchioles are surrounded by tiny bands of smooth muscle. (When these muscles relax, the airways widen; when they contract, the airways narrow.) The inhaled air is then transfered to millions of tiny balloonlike air sacs in the lungs called alveoli. This is where the exchange of oxygen and carbon dioxide takes place.

The main breathing muscle is the diaphragm. This is a dome-shaped sheet of muscle that separates the chest cavity (which holds the heart and lungs) from the abdominal cavity (which holds the stomach and intestines). When you inhale, the diaphragm contracts, moving the "floor" of the chest cavity downward, and the chest muscles lift the rib cage up and outward. This muscle action makes the chest cavity expand and creates a partial vacuum. Air is drawn in through the nose or mouth and down into the lungs. When you exhale, the diaphragm relaxes, raising the floor and making the chest cavity smaller. There is less room for air in the lungs, and it flows up the airways and out through the nose. It seems like inhaling does all the work and exhaling just happens, without the use of any muscles. But in asthmatic lungs, when the air comes in, it becomes trapped, and a person with asthma must struggle to push the air out of the constricted airways.

The airways have a number of built-in defenses to protect the lungs from foreign particles that might be suspended in the air. The nostrils, the openings of the nose, have a fringe of bristly hairs that screen out bugs and other large particles. Tiny pollen grains or particles of dust or soot may get through the first line of defense, but then they are trapped in the sticky fluid, called mucus, produced by the lining of the airways. Some of the lining cells have tiny hairlike structures called cilia. The cilia wave back and forth in coordination, producing currents in the mucus. These currents sweep any trapped particles up and out, keeping them from penetrating deep into the lungs and delivering them to the mouth and nose, where they can be swallowed or coughed or sneezed out.

How Do Asthmatic Lungs Function?

When a person has asthma and the lungs are functioning abnormally, the airways are often described by doctors as hypersensitive or twitchy. Instead of protecting the lungs, the airways overreact when foreign substances are brought in along with the air. The bronchial tubes become irritated and inflamed, causing the bronchial wall to swell. The inflammation causes the bronchial glands to produce an excess amount of mucus, which may form plugs in the bronchi or bronchioles. This adds to the obstruction of the airways. Most important, inflammation leads to hyperresponsiveness. The millions of tiny bands of smooth muscle that are wrapped around the bronchial tubes start to constrict, an effect known as a bronchospasm. The greater the inflammation, the more hyperreactive the airways become. Normal lungs also react to inhaled irritants, but smaller amounts of these substances can trigger constriction in the hyperreactive airways of someone with asthma.

With the flow of air into and out of the lungs restricted, the gas exchange in the alveoli becomes less effective. There is less oxygen to deliver to the body cells, and their waste carbon dioxide builds up in the blood and cells. A higher than normal carbon dioxide concentration in the blood is a key signal for the body's automatic breathing mechanism. The less effectively the person breathes, the more carbon dioxide builds

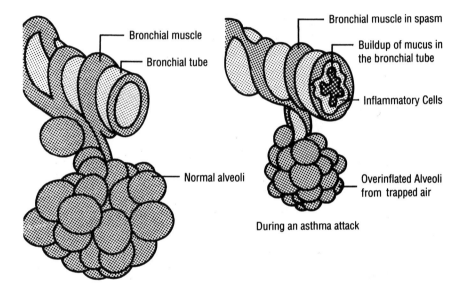

Bronchial muscle

Bronchial tube

Normal alveoli

Bronchial muscle in spasm

Buildup of mucus in the bronchial tube

Inflammatory Cells

Overinflated Alveoli from trapped air

During an asthma attack

During an asthma attack the bronchial tubes of the lungs become irritated and inflamed. An excess amount of mucus is produced forming plugs that obstruct the airways. The bronchial muscles also go into spasm and stale air becomes trapped in the lungs.

up and the stronger the urge to breathe becomes. So an asthma episode leaves people with asthma frightened and desperate for their next breath.

What Are the Symptoms?

Did you ever try breathing through a straw? Many asthma patients say that is what it feels like when they are having an asthma episode. Their narrowing airways force their lungs to work harder to push air through. This sometimes causes them to experience a tightening in the chest. The blocked airways also cause many people with asthma to experience a shortness of breath. Wheezing is the most recognizable symptom of asthma. When the air tries to squeeze through the narrow passageway, it comes with a whistling sound. The sound is produced in the same way as blowing through a whistle. Wheezing is not always apparent in people with asthma, however. That is why asthma often goes undiagnosed. Although wheezing is the most familiar sign of asthma, coughing is actually the most common symptom of this disease. One cause of coughing is the excessive mucus produced by the bronchioles. Bronchospasm alone can also cause coughing. Unfortunately, people often do not see coughing as a sign of something serious like asthma. Instead, it is often overlooked and thought to be the result of a cold. Another sign of an asthma episode is a sucking in of the chest skin. Breathing may be faster, and breathing out may take longer.

Symptoms vary greatly from person to person. Each asthma episode can even be different for the same person. The episodes can be mild, moderate, or severe. It all depends on how seriously the airways are blocked. If the asthma episode is treated quickly and any additional inflammation in the airways is prevented, then only a mild episode may occur. Sometimes, however, inflammation is so severe that it is too late for effective treatment and a trip to the hospital is inevitable. The episode may even lead to death.

Asthma episodes sometimes come in two waves: the early phase and late phase. When the symptoms of the asthma episode appear to be brought under control, this early-phase response has actually set up conditions for a second episode—a stronger one! That is the late-phase response. It is actually a continuation of the first episode. The early-phase response makes the person more vulnerable because during it some of the tiny cilia in the bronchial lining are destroyed. With fewer cilia, the airway lining cannot as effectively clear out the particles of allergens, pollutants, and germs carried in by the inhaled air. They remain trapped in the stagnant mucus, continuing to irritate the delicate airway lining. The late-phase response is often more severe and potentially more dangerous than the early-phase. It can last for a few hours or even a few days if it is not properly treated.

What Triggers Asthma Episodes?

Asthma triggers are things that start the symptoms of an asthma episode. Many of them are substances that can be inhaled, touched, eaten, or injected. Asthma episodes may also be triggered by physical and emotional factors. Regardless of the particular kind of trigger, the reaction is the same. An asthma episode usually occurs immediately or within about fifteen to thirty minutes after exposure to a trigger.

Many experts believe allergies play a major role in asthma. In about 70 percent of asthma cases (and 90 percent of children with asthma), the cause of an asthma episode is an allergy.[3] However, people who have allergies do not necessarily develop asthma. A very common type of allergen is pollen, especially ragweed pollen. Many people have seasonal asthma and have episodes during the "hay fever season."

Other allergens include house dust mites and molds, which can be found all over your house. They accumulate in couches, under mattresses, in closets, in carpets, or in stuffed animals.

Another trigger for people with atopic (allergic) asthma is an allergy to pets. Because the bits of hair shed by pets are very noticeable, most people assume that the hair is the cause of the allergy. Actually, though, the allergens produced by dogs and horses are usually found in their dander (dandruff—the bits of dead skin that flake off). Cats often wash themselves by licking their fur, so people with pet cats may have asthma episodes triggered by exposure not only to cat dander but also to cat saliva. The feathers of birds are also allergenic. As for rodents, such as white mice, guinea pigs, and hamsters, the main allergen is in their urine. Another animal that can cause allergy problems is not a pet but a pest—many people are allergic to substances in cockroach feces.[4]

Pollution can be a powerful trigger of asthma episodes. Living in an urban area can be very hard on an asthmatic.

Many people are allergic to substances in cockroach feces.

Exhaust from cars, fumes coming from factories, and cigarette smoke can all be irritating to already sensitive airways. Even secondhand smoke can be harmful to a person with asthma. So if you are a parent of a child with asthma, your child's health is the best reason in the whole world to quit smoking. The new laws stating that smokers cannot light up in specific public places have allowed asthmatics to breathe a little easier.

As many as 50 to 60 percent of adult asthma patients have breathing problems after taking aspirin or other painkillers such as ibuprofen (Motrin®, Advil®, Nuprin®, etc.). Even the smallest amount of these could send a susceptible person to the hospital with a severe asthma episode. Acetaminophen (Tylenol®) is a good substitute because it does not aggravate asthma symptoms. Ironically, the painkillers that can act as asthma triggers also have anti-inflammatory activity, but acetaminophen does not.

Foods, whether eaten or inhaled, can bring on an asthma episode. Such common foods as milk products, fish, nuts, wheat, or eggs can cause an allergic reaction.

Some people are allergic to food additives, including dyes and preservatives such as sulfites. Sulfites are often added to foods we order in restaurants, especially salads. They are also frequently added to products we buy in the store.

Some nonallergic asthma triggers include weather conditions. Cold or dry air can cause an episode to occur. Weather extremes from hot to cold or vice versa can bring on an episode as well. Walking out of your warm, cozy house into cold, wintry weather can make the bronchial tubes constrict, causing problems for the airways.

Viral infections, caused by the common cold or flu, are common triggers among children and adults. Viral infections in the lungs can damage the respiratory lining and can also increase bronchial sensitivity.[5]

In the past, stress and emotional factors were widely believed to be the cause of asthma. Medical specialists now realize that emotions do not *cause* asthma, but they can trigger an asthma episode. Strong emotional reactions, such as crying and even laughing, can also be asthma triggers.

Exercise is a very common nonallergic trigger for people with asthma. When people exercise, their muscles use up extra oxygen. So their lungs work harder, breathing faster and taking in more air than when they are inactive. The nose is unable to purify and warm all the air that enters the lungs during exercise, as it does under normal conditions. The untreated air, which may be cold and dry, then goes directly into the trachea and lungs. This causes the air passages to dry out and lose the moist blanket of mucus that normally protects them. Since people with asthma have hypersensitive air passages, dry air is more likely to cause an asthma episode. Doctors call this problem exercise-induced asthma (EIA) or exercise-induced bronchospasm (EIB). Approximately 80 to 90 percent of people with asthma have EIA. However, people with EIA should not give up exercising because they are afraid of triggering asthma episodes. In fact, in the 1984 summer Olympics, sixty-seven members of the United States Olympic

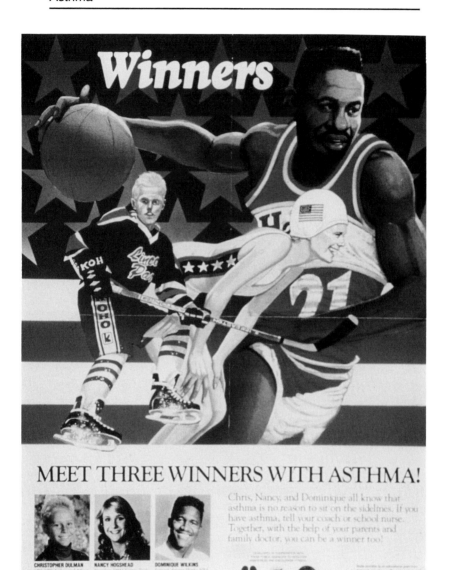

People with asthma do not have to give up exercising. With proper diagnosis and treatment athletes can continue to compete. In fact, many gold medal Olympians have asthma.

Team experienced exercise-induced asthma at one time or another. Some well-known athletes who have asthma include runner Jackie Joyner-Kersee, swimmer Nancy Hogshead, and diver Greg Louganis—EIA did not stop these athletes from winning Olympic gold medals. In the 1984 summer Olympics, the sixty-seven athletes with asthma won forty-one medals! They all worked out their own ways of managing their asthma. Many of them relied on a combination of warm-ups and medication.[6]

How Do We Get Allergies?

Allergies are an overreaction of a particular part of the immune system. The immune system's job is to protect the body from any foreign invaders, such as disease germs. The immune system is equipped with an army of soldiers, the white blood cells. They travel in the bloodstream and can even slip through the gaps between body cells. Our white cell defenders are always on guard, ready to attack invaders. They recognize them by the unfamiliar proteins or other chemicals on their surface— chemicals that are not found on normal body cells. When a foreign chemical has been identified, some specialized immune cells produce proteins called antibodies that react with the foreign chemicals. The antibodies may damage an invading germ or make it easier for the white blood cells to catch and kill. After the battle is over, some of these specialized antibodies are kept in the body. Then, if the same kind of germ invades again, the antibodies against it can be used as patterns to quickly manufacture a new supply of ammunition against it. This time the person is immune to that disease and does not become ill.

Unfortunately, some people's immune systems are a little too active and produce antibodies against chemicals that would not have caused any harm to their bodies. These foreign chemicals may be on the surface of pollen grains or other particles breathed in with the air or in foods; drugs such as penicillin can also stimulate an immune reaction. The antibodies produced against these chemicals are of a special kind called immunoglobulin E (IgE). This is the sort of antibody normally produced against parasites, such as the pinworms that can live in human intestines. (The antibodies produced against disease germs are mainly of a different type, called immunoglobulin G or IgG.) Some medical experts believe that more people have allergies these days because improved sanitation has made internal parasites rare in the developed countries. So a body system that once was important for people's survival has been left with nothing to do—except cause trouble.

Substances that stimulate unnecessary IgE production are called allergens because they result in an allergic reaction. Each kind of allergen stimulates the production of specialized IgE antibodies, which normally will react only with that particular allergen. The effects of this reaction, which are far more harmful to the body than the allergens themselves, are actually due to misguided efforts of the body's own defenders.

A person with asthma produces a large amount of IgE antibodies, more than a normal person. These antibodies attach to

ASTHMA DRUGS IN SPORTS

Athletes with exercise-induced asthma (EIA) depend on asthma medication to help them get through strenuous activities. But sometimes taking medication in sports can cause problems for athletes, even when they use only legal drugs, prescribed by a physician, or over-the-counter drugs such as cold remedies. The United States Olympic Committee has a drug hotline, 1-800-233-0393, to advise on which drugs are permitted and which can be substituted for drugs on the banned list. The Olympic drug rules can be tricky—the drugs theophylline and cromolyn are allowed, for example, but other asthma drugs, albuterol and terbutaline, are permitted only in aerosol form, not in tablets or syrup. Failure to follow all the rules can have dreadful consequences, as United States swimmer Dick DeMont found out in the 1972 Olympics. He lost his Olympic gold medal because he did not file for approval of his anti-EIA medication. Because he did not declare his asthma drugs, he was accused of "doping."

special immune system cells called mast cells, found in the skin and in the linings of the respiratory and digestive tracts. There they act as guards, on the alert against invading parasites and other suspicious particles.

When challenged by an allergen—ragweed pollen breathed into the nose, for example—the mast cells with their IgE antibodies are stimulated and mobilize a multipronged attack. The mast cells become "leaky" and release strong chemicals called mediators into the surrounding tissues. The mediators summon white blood cells and also cause inflammation: The surrounding tissues become swollen and watery, and the mucus-producing cells step up their slime production. The person having the allergic reaction experiences the discomfort of a stuffy, runny nose, but actually inflammation would have some benefits if the body were fighting a real threat. The extra mucus would help trap the invading particles, and white blood cells can move more easily through swollen, watery tissues. The allergy mediators may also cause bronchospasm, a contraction of the airway muscles, narrowing the breathing passages. The best known of the allergy mediators is histamine. Drugs called antihistamines combat allergic reactions by blocking the action of histamine. They do this by tying up the receptors where histamine normally binds to the surface of cells. So even when there is plenty of histamine in the blood, the susceptible cells do not receive the inflammatory message.

During the very first encounter with a particular allergen, such as ragweed pollen, a susceptible person may not experience any allergic symptoms. However, the white blood cells

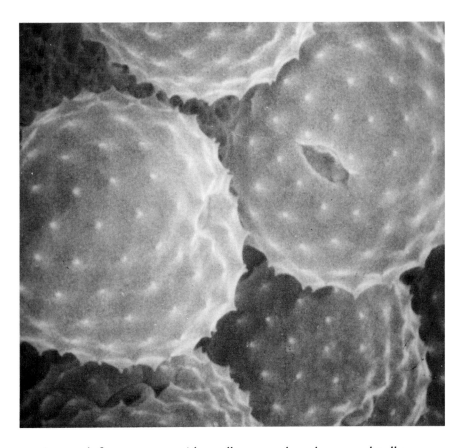

A person's first encounter with an allergen, such as the ragweed pollen shown here (magnified 3,000 times), may not produce any allergic symptoms. With each exposure, however, more antibodies are produced and the symptoms become worse.

have now identified the foreign substance, and specific IgE antibodies are produced against it. Each new exposure boosts the production of specialized IgE antibodies—so the more frequently one is exposed to the specific allergen, the worse the symptoms will be.

Nighttime Asthma

"For years my children's asthma kept us awake and frightened night after night, only to 'disappear' by the time we would see the doctor the next day," relates Debbie Scherrer, the mother of two children with asthma.[7] She was tired of hearing her children wheeze and cough, tired of having the doctor look at her as though she was either crazy or overprotective, and just plain tired from all the nights of lost sleep, when she finally attended a patient education workshop and heard Dr. Guillermo Mendoza explain just what was happening to her family. Lung function, like most of the other body functions, goes in cycles, depending on the time of day. The lungs typically work best in the afternoon, then become gradually less effective as the day goes on, reaching a low point between midnight and 6 A.M. Doctors are not completely sure why this happens, but part of the reason appears to be that the body's natural production of hormones such as adrenaline and cortisone drops during the night. Moreover, when people lie down to sleep, mucus tends to pool and accumulate in their airways. When the airways are hyperreactive, an asthma episode can result. Nighttime asthma is especially common in children—and very hard on their parents! The child wakes up, wheezing and coughing and scared. The parents come running and give medications, warm liquids to drink, and reassuring hugs while trying to hide the fact that they are very worried. By the time the doctor has office hours, though, the child has recovered. Lung function is now nearing its peak; the doctor hears quiet breathing and clear lungs and may wonder if the parents are exaggerating the problem. So the child does not receive adequate treatment, and the nighttime episodes continue. Fortunately, there are now better methods of diagnosing asthma than just listening through a stethoscope.

4

Diagnosing Asthma

Seventeen-year-old Krissy Taylor had a bright future in modeling, like her supermodel sister, Niki Taylor. But when Niki found Krissy lying on the living room floor of her family's home in early July 1995, that future came to a tragic end. For weeks, no one could figure out what had caused Krissy's death. There was no sign of alcohol, amphetamines, cocaine, or any other kind of drugs in her blood. The only thing they knew for certain was that Krissy had taken the over-the-counter asthma drug Primatene Mist®, just a couple of hours before her death. This drug contains the hormone adrenaline, which is known to speed up the heartbeat. Krissy took the drug because she had complained of a shortness of breath that she attributed to stress. Her doctor had never diagnosed her as having asthma. It was not until several weeks after her death that the cause was finally revealed. When a pathologist looked through a microscope at tissue samples from Krissy's body, he noticed that her bronchioles were inflamed and scarred, indicating that she did indeed have asthma.

Unaware of the seriousness of her breathing problems, Krissy had tried to treat it herself. She had ignored warnings on the Primatene Mist® label, stating that the inhaler should be used only if a doctor has diagnosed asthma. The inhaler gave Krissy temporary relief, but it may have masked the severity of her problem. "Every time people use these over-the-counter remedies, they are delaying getting long-term care," explains Dr. William Busse of the University of Wisconsin Medical School. If only Krissy or her family had realized how sick she was, her death could have been prevented, and she could have received proper treatment.[1]

The Masquerader

Unfortunately, all too often doctors are unable to make a proper diagnosis of asthma. Asthma is a tricky disease. Many of its symptoms are commonly confused with those of other respiratory illnesses, such as emphysema, chronic bronchitis, heart disease, blood clots in the lung, and cystic fibrosis. People with these diseases may experience wheezing, coughing, shortness of breath, chest tightness, and general breathing difficulties—all symptoms of asthma.

Why is it so important to distinguish asthma from these other diseases? Of all the respiratory diseases mentioned in the last paragraph, treatments for asthma are the most effective,

Failure to diagnose asthma can lead to deadly results, such as incorrect medication. The death of model Krissy Taylor in July 1995 was the result of an over-the-counter asthma medication. She had never been diagnosed with asthma and her condition was not confirmed until after her death.

and with proper treatment, asthma patients have the best chances of recovering to lead a long and normal life. Therefore, a proper diagnosis of asthma can ensure the best possible treatment with a very positive outlook.

Collect Information

There are a number of things that can be done to form an accurate diagnosis of asthma. The first thing the physician needs to do is to collect a history of the illness. Simply listing symptoms does not guarantee a proper diagnosis. Therefore, a more thorough investigation of the illness is needed. A complete diagnosis includes a five-step process:

1) The first step is to collect a personal and family history. A family history of allergy could be an indication of asthma. Also, a medication history is important. If you take aspirin, that could be an asthma trigger.

2) The second step is to inform the doctor of when the illness began.

3) The third step is to get a clear idea of the current complaints. What are the symptoms? When do you experience them? Does the problem worsen during laughter, crying, or after exercising? How severe are the episodes?

4) The fourth step is to discuss previous treatment and results. What kind of drugs have you taken to help your symptoms? Did your condition improve, worsen, or stay the same?

NOT ALL THAT WHEEZES IS ASTHMA

Wheezing, shortness of breath, and a tightness in the throat sound like obvious signs of asthma, right? These also happen to be typical symptoms of another illness, called vocal cord dysfunction (VCD), in which the vocal cords do not open wide during breathing. Unlike those with asthma, VCD patients do not show any change in oxygen levels during attacks, and they do not have nighttime attacks. The vocal cord problem can be diagnosed by actually looking into the larynx (the voice box) with a flexible probe called a fiberoptic laryngoscope. Doctors stress that both diseases can coexist, but if only the VCD is diagnosed, the asthma treatment can be stopped.[2]

5) The last step is to inform the doctor of any life-threatening complications. About 10 percent of severe asthma patients will experience a life-threatening episode at least once a year.

Physical Examination

Once the physician has collected information from the patient, the next step is a physical examination. The doctor will first check for wheezing, using a stethoscope. Although wheezing is a very recognizable symptom, it is present only when the patient is actually having an episode. Sometimes no wheezing is heard at all, even during an episode. Therefore, the next step is to check the breathing muscles to see if they appear overused, which is another sign of asthma. These are indications that airway obstruction exists, but they do not distinguish asthma from other respiratory diseases. Therefore, further testing is necessary.

Chest X-rays

Chest X-rays can also confirm airway obstruction, especially when they are taken while the patient is having breathing difficulties. If the problem is pneumonia, tuberculosis, or

THE ASTHMA THAT WASN'T

A Hong Kong physician, Dr. Robert Tseng, reported in the *New England Journal of Medicine* on a five-year-old boy who had been having nighttime asthma episodes for two months and also coughed after exercise. A month of treatment with anti-inflammatory and bronchodilator drugs helped the cough, but the boy was still wheezing. The boy's father recalled that the child had swallowed a small part from his Lego® set a few months before. Nothing abnormal showed up on several tests. Then a radioisotope scan finally showed an obstruction in the left bronchus. Using a bronchoscope, a surgeon fished out a 0.5-cm Lego piece, and the wheezing stopped.[3]

some other lung disorder, the X-rays will show characteristic changes in the lungs. The lungs of a person with asthma usually look normal between episodes, however, unless there has been some previous damage.

Blood Tests

Blood samples are analyzed to get various kinds of useful information. For example, the different types of blood cells are identified and counted to give a blood count. Some people with asthma have an unusually high number of eosinophils. These are specialized white blood cells that attack invading parasites or flock to the site of an allergic reaction. Eosinophils release inflammatory chemicals, causing much of the tissue damage that occurs during an asthma episode. Blood tests can also determine whether the person has any other disease that might complicate the treatment of asthma.

Sputum Analysis

People with a chronic cough often cough up a substance called sputum, which contains mucus and some foreign particles. A sputum analysis is made by looking at the sputum under a microscope. In specimens from asthmatic patients, the analysis may indicate the presence of eosinophils, along with bits of destroyed cells, fragments of mold, and mucus plugs still holding the shape of the small airways in which they formed.

Spirometry or Pulmonary Function Tests

Measurements of lung function can indicate the presence of airway obstruction as well as the severity of the problem. One group of tests is called lung volume measurements. They measure the amount of air taken into the lungs at different points in the breathing cycle. The measurements are taken with an instrument called a spirometer. The patient breathes into a mouthpiece connected by a tube to a machine that measures the volumes of air breathed in and out and plots the results on a graph.

Various kinds of useful information can be obtained from these tests. The vital capacity (VC) is determined by having the person first inhale as deeply as possible then exhale as much air as possible. The VC is usually about 80 percent of the total lung volume. (Some air always remains in the lungs, no matter how hard one tries to blow it out.) A VC lower than this indicates a breathing problem, but, by itself, cannot establish what kind. In another spirometer test, the person is told to breathe in deeply, then breathe out forcefully as fast as possible. This test gives a value called the forced vital capacity (FVC). Because the spirometer plots the volumes on a time scale, it is also possible to determine the amounts of air exhaled after specific periods of time (after one second, for example). These values are called the forced expiratory volume (FEV) ("expiration" is the technical term for exhaling); FEV would be the amount of air exhaled after one second. The FVC and FEV values and their ratio give an indication of whether the airways are narrowed and can indicate inflammation.

Repeating the tests after inhaling a bronchodilator provides further information about the state of the airways. Spirometry is useful for diagnosing asthma and evaluating its severity. Repeating the tests at regular intervals helps in monitoring the response to therapy.[4]

Another group of pulmonary tests is called ventilation measurements. Some of these tests measure the resistance encountered by air being breathed in and out. When airways are blocked, the resistance is greatly increased—often to seven to ten times greater than normal and sometimes even up to twenty-five times the normal resistance.[5] The tests in this group also include measurements of airflow—the amount of air entering or leaving the lungs in a specific time.

A key clue to establishing a diagnosis of asthma is the fact that it is reversible—although the airways are blocked during an episode, they go back to normal afterward. This can be established by running two sets of pulmonary tests. First an asthma episode is provoked, using a drug (usually methacholine or histamine) or one of the patient's known triggers such as exercise or cold air. (Using an allergen or irritant for a provocation test can be very dangerous, even with the doctor standing by. It is not used for routine diagnosis of asthma, only to establish an environmental cause—for example, an air pollutant in the workplace.) After the first set of pulmonary tests is run, a bronchodilator is given to bring the person's airways back to normal, and the same tests are run

There are many methods used for diagnosing asthma. This woman is using a nebulizer to inhale a bronchodilator that will bring her airways back to normal after an asthma episode was provoked during a series of pulmonary tests.

again. If the first tests show airway obstruction and the second set shows a marked improvement in the air flow, then a diagnosis of asthma can be made. The severity of the episode and its response to the bronchodilator help the doctor develop a treatment plan tailor-made to the patient's needs.

Allergy Testing

Since allergies are among the most common triggers of asthma, allergy testing is another important diagnostic technique. The purpose of the tests is to identify the allergens responsible for provoking an asthma episode. Skin testing detects IgE-mediated responses. (Mast cells in the skin contain some of the same kinds of specific IgE antibodies as the sensitized mast cells in the airways.) In the intracutaneous test, small amounts of specific allergens are injected into the skin; if the person is sensitive to a particular allergen, a wheal (a raised area) surrounded by a reddened area soon forms at the spot where the allergen was injected. In another variation, the prick test, a drop of allergen-containing solution is placed on the surface of the skin, and then the upper layers of skin are pricked with a needle, introducing a tiny amount of the allergen. The prick test is much less sensitive than the intracutaneous test, but when the person is extremely sensitive, it is much safer, less likely to provoke a very serious reaction. When skin tests cannot be given, perhaps because the patient has a severe skin rash or is taking antihistamines, doctors can use a method called the radioallergosorbent test

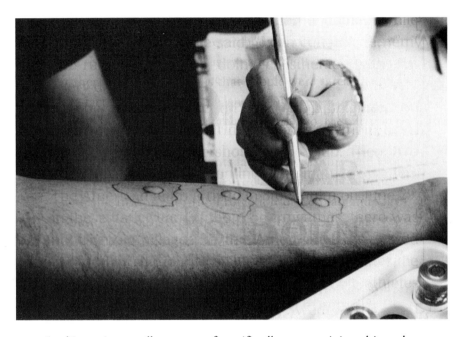

In skin testing, small amounts of specific allergens are injected into the skin. A raised area known as a wheal, surrounded by a reddened area, forms if the person is sensitive to a particular allergen.

(RAST). RAST tests for specific IgE antibodies in a sample of the patient's blood, but it is less sensitive than skin tests.

Peak Flow Meter

There is one diagnostic method that asthma patients can use in their own home. This technique involves a convenient, hand-held device called the peak flow meter. This device measures the speed at which air flows out of the lungs during the first 150 milliseconds when a person exhales rapidly. When the reading indicates a drop in the airflow, this is a sign of bronchospasm—an asthma episode may be developing. The airflow change occurs before the person has any conscious awareness of breathing difficulty. So peak flow meters are perfect early warning devices that can show that an episode is coming before it actually happens—in time to take preventive measures. Doctors recommend using the peak flow meter routinely, first thing in the morning and just before bedtime. This is a very popular device for people capable of self-monitoring their asthma.

A peak flow meter can be especially valuable in diagnosing cases of nighttime asthma. It can save mothers like Debbie Scherrer a lot of unnecessary frustration. Her children's doctor was not very knowledgeable about asthma. If he had used a peak flow meter, Scherrer points out, "he would have been able to tell that my 'perfectly fine' child was operating at about only 80 percent of his breathing capacity."[6] She could also have taken readings at home, during the episodes, and thus

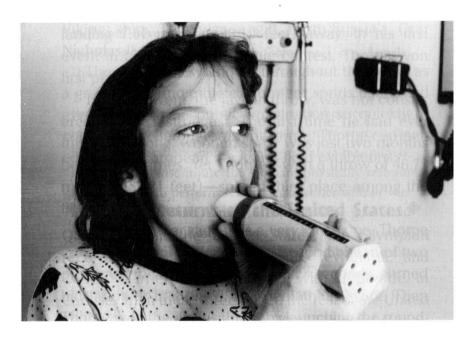

A peak flow meter can be used to measure the speed at which air flows out of the lungs when a person exhales rapidly. A drop in airflow may indicate that an asthma episode is developing.

could have given the doctor all the information needed to draw up an effective treatment plan.

Regular use of a peak flow meter can be a lifesaver. In a study of eleven asthma patients who had nearly died from asthma episodes, compared with asthma patients who had never had such serious episodes and people without asthma, researchers found that those who had had near-fatal episodes were less aware of shortness of breath and other signs of breathing difficulties. Their bodies were also less able to adjust for a low oxygen supply by increasing the heart and breathing rates. Monitoring with a peak flow meter can pick up episodes in the early stages, when they are more easily treated.[7]

The Asthma Diary

One very important tool in self-management is to keep a diary of all aspects of the asthma. When does it occur? What are the symptoms? What was the person doing before it happened? These are some important questions that can help an asthmatic get a clearer picture of his or her disease. This asthma diary will allow asthmatics and their doctors to understand their illness better. Therefore, they will be able to treat their asthma more effectively.

Severity of Symptoms

Once a person has been diagnosed with asthma, it is very important for the physician to be able to classify the severity of the symptoms in order to draw up an effective treatment plan.

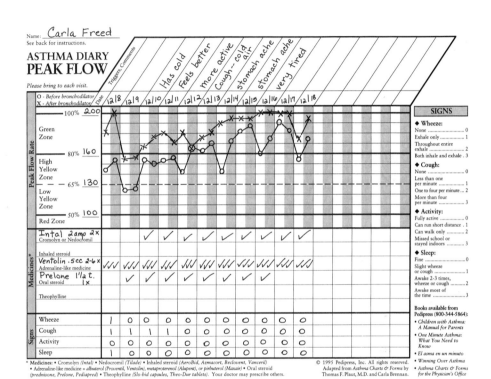

Name: **Carla Freed**
See back for instructions.

ASTHMA DIARY
PEAK FLOW

Please bring to each visit.

Triggers, Comments

Has cold / Feels better / More active / Cough - cold air / stomach ache / stomach ache / very tired

O - Before bronchodilator
X - After bronchodilator

Date: 12|8 / 12|9 / 12|10 / 12|11 / 12|12 / 12|13 / 12|14 / 12|15 / 12|16 / 12|17 / 12|18

Peak Flow Rate			
100% **200**	Green Zone		
80% **160**	High Yellow Zone		
65% **130**	Low Yellow Zone		
50% **100**	Red Zone		

SIGNS

◆ Wheeze:
None 0
Exhale only 1
Throughout entire
exhale 2
Both inhale and exhale . 3

◆ Cough:
None 0
Less than one
per minute 1
One to four per minute ... 2
More than four
per minute 3

◆ Activity:
Fully active 0
Can run short distance . 1
Can walk only 2
Missed school or
stayed indoors 3

◆ Sleep:
Fine 0
Slight wheeze
or cough 1
Awake 2-3 times,
wheeze or cough 2
Awake most of
the time 3

Medicines*

	12	8	12	9	12	10	12	11	12	12	12	13	12	14	12	15	12	16	12	17	12	18
Intal 2 amp 2x Cromolyn or Nedocomil		✓	✓	✓	✓	✓	✓	✓	✓	✓	
Inhaled steroid											
Ventolin .5cc 2-6x Adrenaline-like medicine	✓✓✓	✓✓✓	✓✓✓	✓✓✓	✓✓✓	✓✓✓	✓✓✓	✓✓✓	✓✓✓	✓✓✓	✓✓✓
Prelone 1½ t. 1x Oral steroid		✓	✓	✓	✓	✓	✓	✓			
Theophylline											

Books available from
Pedipress (800-344-5864):
• *Children with Asthma:*
A Manual for Parents
• *One Minute Asthma:*
What You Need to
Know
• *El asma en un minuto*
• *Winning Over Asthma*
• *Asthma Charts & Forms*
for the Physician's Office

Signs

	12	8	12	9	12	10	12	11	12	12	12	13	12	14	12	15	12	16	12	17	12	18
Wheeze	1	O	O	O	O	O	O	O	O	O	O
Cough	1	1	1	1	O	O	O	O	O	O	O
Activity	O	O	O	O	O	O	O	O	O	O	O
Sleep	1	O	O	O	O	O	O	O	O	O	O

* **Medicines:** • Cromolyn *(Intal)* • Nedocromil *(Tilade)* • Inhaled steroid *(AeroBid, Azmacort, Beclovent, Vanceril)*
• Adrenaline-like medicine = albuterol *(Proventil, Ventolin)*, metaproterenol *(Alupent)*, or pirbuterol *(Maxair)* • Oral steroid
(prednisone, Prelone, Pediapred) • Theophylline *(Slo-bid capsules, Theo-Dur tablets)*. Your doctor may prescribe others.

© 1995 Pedipress, Inc. All rights reserved.
Adapted from *Asthma Charts & Forms* by
Thomas F. Plaut, M.D. and Carla Brennan.

Keeping a diary of all aspects of asthma symptoms is an important tool
in self-management.

Researchers have found that patients, their relatives, and even health care professionals often underestimate the severity of asthma symptoms. The results of lung function tests provide a more objective assessment. Asthma specialists currently distinguish four stages of severity of the disorder: mild intermittent, mild persistent, moderate persistent, and severe persistent.

In mild intermittent asthma, episodes are irritating but do not interfere with daily activities. They occur less than once a week, and there is less than a 20 percent drop in peak flow or FEV. Episodes are brief (from a few hours to a few days), and nighttime symptoms occur less than twice a month. Between episodes, the patients have no symptoms, and their lung functions are normal or within 80 percent of normal. Asthma medication is needed only occasionally, and there is no need to take anti-inflammatory medications on a continuous basis. Dr. Arthur Torre, a specialist in asthma in children and adolescents, points out that many people think they fit into this category but actually have symptoms more often than the definition of this category allows. Underestimating the severity of the asthma can lead to undertreatment. Then the inflammation increases the airway hyperresponsiveness, and the asthma gets worse.[8]

In mild persistent asthma, the peak flows are normal or nearly normal, but episodes occur more than once a week (but less than once a day). Nighttime symptoms also occur more often, more than twice a month.

Even one of the following features will classify asthma as moderate persistent: daily symptoms (even coughing) or symptoms that interfere with daily activities or with sleep (with nighttime symptoms more than once a week) or the use of short-acting bronchodilators each day to make breathing easier. Long-term asthma medication is needed. Dr. Torre notes that many patients in the moderate category do not realize they have asthma. They have coughing episodes several times a week, especially after exercise and at night but think the cause is postnasal drip. Pulmonary function tests show significant changes.[9]

Patients with severe persistent asthma have continuous symptoms and peak flows or FEV values 60 percent of normal or less. Severe episodes, with drops in the peak flow of 30 percent or more, result in almost daily restriction of activities, and nighttime episodes also occur often. The right combintion of treatment measures can help these patients, too, to bring their asthma under control. As Dr. Torre notes, "Control consists of minimal (ideally no) chronic symptoms including nocturnal; normal exercise tolerance; infrequent episodes; no emergency visits; and minimal (less than two or three times a week) need for . . . bronchodilator therapy."[10]

5

Treatment of Asthma

I magine a group of eight to ten Greeks, around the end of the second century A.D., dressed in togas and sandals. They have just sailed the treacherous seas from their homeland to the island of Sicily. Once they arrived, they proceeded to hike up 10,902-foot-high Mt. Etna. This feat would have been difficult enough for anyone, but imagine that these hikers had asthma. Those who managed to make it to the top, wheezing all the way, were greeted by an active volcano blowing out sulfuric smoke that irritated the hikers' already hypersensitive airways. Their bronchioles were filling up with mucus and clogging up the airways, making them gasp desperately for air. That sounds pretty horrifying, but it was actually the treatment for asthma prescribed by the Greek physician Galen. The sulphurous fumes were supposed to act as an expectorant, loosening the mucus in the airways so it could be coughed and spit out. (The ancient accounts that describe this treatment do not give any statistics on how many of Galen's patients managed to get off the mountain alive.)[1]

Galen's treatment would not be very popular today. Fortunately, there has been a great deal of progress in asthma treatment since then. Although there is currently no cure for asthma, there are various effective treatments available that make it possible for asthma patients to live normal, fulfilling lives.

Self-Management Is the Key to Treatment

Asthma is similar to diabetes: They are both chronic conditions in which the patients play a major role in the management and treatment of the illness. Self-management is the key to controlling asthma. With the guidance of their physicians, asthmatics can take back control of their lives. These days, asthma devices are made especially for the patients' convenience. For instance, the peak flow meter, as described in the preceding chapter, is a handy gadget people can use to find out when an episode is coming so they can treat it before they experience symptoms.

There are two basic ways of treating mild asthma. One is to take medication to treat the asthma symptoms. The other is to take asthma drugs before exposure to a trigger in order to prevent the onset of an episode. It is important to use the least amount of medication necessary to achieve the desired results. Moderate and severe asthma also requires daily anti-inflammatory medication.

Inhalers Are Popular in Asthma Treatment

Asthma drugs come in many forms: tablets, liquids, inhalants, injections, and gels. Medications that require injections are usually administered primarily by a physician. The other forms can be used by the patient with the doctor's guidance. However, inhalers are the most popular device used for asthma treatment because they are fast, easy, and convenient.

The type of inhaler that most people use is a hand-held device. There are several different kinds of inhalers, some more complicated than others. The inhaler sprays a mist of medication directly into the person's bronchial tubes. From there, it is able to open up the airways and relieve the symptoms. It is estimated that a typical inhaler allows only about 10 percent of the inhaled drug into the lungs. The remaining 90 percent stays on the lining of the mouth and throat. But the 10 percent that does penetrate into the lungs is enough to get the desired effect.[2] The use of a spacer can make the inhaler easier to use and more effective. With a spacer device, the drug first passes into a chamber where particles of the medication are held in suspension for three to five seconds. The patient can inhale the drug during this time. With a spacer, more of the drug gets into the lungs (15 percent), and only 35 percent is deposited in the mouth and throat. (The rest stays in the spacer.)[3]

Inhalers are fairly simple, hand-held devices that are beneficial as long as they are used correctly. Even children are able to use them, especially when they include a spacer and a face mask. Asthma medication used to be given primarily through injection, and many children were so afraid of getting shots that they did not even tell their parents when they were getting an asthma episode. Now children do not have to fear asthma treatment. However, many schools do not allow children to keep their inhalers with them. They are required to leave the device at the nurse's office. The problem is, asthma episodes usually need immediate attention, and too much time is wasted by the time they reach the nurse's off ce. Some states have passed laws to change this policy.

The Treatment Plan Depends on Severity

The goal of all asthma treatment is to bring the disorder under control, restoring normal lung function and minimizing or eliminating symptoms. How this can be achieved depends on how severe the asthma is.

Mild intermittent asthma can generally be controlled by treating the occasional episodes with inhaled bronchodilators, drugs that open up (dilate) the narrowed airways (bronchioles). But if the patient begins having episodes more often than once a week or so or if the lung function values fall by more than 20 percent, the asthma has progressed to a more severe stage, mild persistent asthma. Then additional measures are needed to keep the condition from getting worse.

Mild persistent asthma calls for treatment with "controllers," drugs to combat inflammation and help keep the disorder under control. At this stage, an anti-inflammatory drug such as cromolyn is taken daily. Efforts to avoid asthma triggers can also be helpful. In addition, short-acting bronchodilators are used to treat episodes, and long-acting bronchodilators may be used at night. It takes a couple of weeks for the anti-inflammatory medication to become fully effective. After that the bronchodilators should be needed only a few times a week.

Moderate persistent asthma calls for stronger measures. Generally, inhaled steroids (stronger anti-inflammatory drugs than cromolyn) are used as daily controller medications. Measures to eliminate potential asthma triggers from the patient's environment are very important. Allergy shots to reduce the person's sensitivity to particular allergens can also be useful. Bronchodilators are used to treat episodes, but, as asthma specialist Dr. Arthur Torre notes:

> Our goal is to reduce the *need* for "rescue" medication to several times a day, and ideally to only several times a week. Remember the more inflammation, the more variable the pulmonary functions will be, and the more frequent and severe the symptoms will be. The basic strategy then is to use "enough" anti-inflammatory therapy so the moderate persistent patient *on* medication will essentially be similar to the mild episodic patient *off* medication.[4]

Severe persistent asthma requires even stronger measures. A combination of controller medications including high-dose

There are many types of devices that can be used to treat asthma depending on the severity of the condition.

inhaled steroids is taken daily. Long-acting bronchodilators are also used. Oral corticosteroids may be given for seven to fourteen days to decrease the inflammation and make the airways more responsive to bronchodilators.

Bronchodilators' Role in Asthma

Bronchodilators are drugs often used to relieve asthma symptoms, although they can also be used to prevent episodes as well. They may be taken through a special inhaler that goes directly into the bronchial tubes. There are three leading types of bronchodilators: adrenergic, anticholinergic, and theophylline.

Adrenergic drugs, also known as beta-2 agonists, work like adrenaline, the hormone produced by the adrenal gland. Doctors use adrenergic drugs as their first choice in an emergency because they work fast and open up the bronchioles in just minutes. In the past, a shot of epinephrine (adrenaline) was the standard treatment for anyone who ended up in the emergency room with an asthma episode. Adrenaline used to be available only in a form for injection. These days, adrenergic drugs can be taken using inhalers.

Anticholinergic drugs are used to block the production of acetylcholine, a mediator chemical produced by the vagus nerve, which helps control the functions of the lungs. Increased activity of the vagus nerve is believed to be involved in the airway hyperreactivity that leads to an asthma episode. Anticholinergic drugs cause the bronchial muscles to relax when they become constricted. These drugs also dry up excess mucus.

Theophylline was the most widely prescribed oral asthma medication in the United States for thirty years. It is not available as an inhalant. Theophylline has properties similar to caffeine, which is found naturally in coffee, tea, and colas and is added to many other soft drinks. (In an emergency, if no asthma drugs are on hand, drinking a cup of coffee can help relieve asthma symptoms.) Theophylline differs from other bronchodilators in that it is a slow-acting drug. It does not help stop an asthma episode because it takes too long to become effective. Instead, it is used regularly as a maintenance medication. The dose of this drug must be carefully adjusted for each patient, and its concentration in the blood must be monitored periodically. Theophylline can cause serious side effects—nausea and vomiting, a fast and irregular heartbeat, and sometimes seizures and even death. With the many newer drugs now available, theophylline is used much less than it used to be.

Corticosteroids

Corticosteroids, usually just called steroids, are asthma drugs that are derived from cortisol, a natural hormone produced by the adrenal gland in the body. Steroids relieve symptoms in almost all asthma patients. They block the production and release of inflammatory chemicals, relax the airway muscles, and decrease mucus production. The effects are quick and dramatic for acute episodes. However, steroids are powerful drugs with terrible side effects. They can stunt the growth of children and cause osteoporosis (a weakening of the bones) in adults; they may cause the skin to thin and bruise easily, weaken the muscles, cause obesity, lead to diabetes, cause high blood pressure, and dangerously weaken the body's defenses against bacterial and viral infections. With all these negatives, for a long time doctors used steroid drugs only in an emergency, never to be taken on a regular basis. That is still the case for steroids taken by mouth, but the newer synthetic corticosteroids can be inhaled as aerosols. Taken this way, they have fewer side effects while still producing a powerful effect where they are needed, in the airways. Inhaled steroids that

 # STEROIDS AS MUSCLE BUILDERS

Asthma patients sometimes confuse the steroids their doctor prescribes to treat their asthma with the steroids that produce huge muscles. Actually, there are many kinds of steroids. Some are hormones, made naturally in the body. The steroid hormones include sex hormones and hormones that help regulate the body's use of minerals and sugar. The illegal drugs that are sometimes used by athletes, called anabolic steroids, are similar to male sex hormones. They are very different from the anti-inflammatory drugs legally prescribed to people suffering from respiratory diseases.

can be taken every day include beclomethasone, flunisolide, budesonide, and triamcinolone—but even these should be taken on a long-term basis only under the careful supervision of a doctor.

Cromolyn Sodium

Cromolyn sodium works in a different way from other anti-asthma drugs. It is not a bronchodilator, and it does not block the production or action of histamine and other mast-cell mediators. It works by preventing the mast cells from releasing inflammatory mediators when they are stimulated by allergens. Cromolyn sodium thus can prevent asthma episodes but cannot help an episode once it has already started. It is the safest drug used to treat asthma in children.

Nedocromil is a newer drug with some chemical similarities to cromolyn. When inhaled, it reduces airway inflammation in several ways. Nedocromil blocks the activation not only of mast cells but also of eosinophils and other kinds of white blood cells involved in the inflammatory reaction, and it prevents their release of histamine and other mediators.

The Timing Counts

Scientists have known for a long time that the body has natural cycles that occur each day with clocklike regularity. The levels of hormones and other chemicals rise and fall over each twenty-four-hour span, and so does the body temperature. Cyclic changes in the body make us fall asleep at night, wake up in the morning, and tend to feel a bit groggy in midafternoon. There are also particular times in the daily cycle when babies are most likely to be born (in the morning) and when heart attacks are most likely to occur (around 6 A.M.). Asthma episodes, too, have their own typical timing. They are most likely to occur at night, between midnight and 6 A.M., when airway inflammation is the worst. Recently medical specialists and drug researchers have begun to apply this knowledge to determine when medications should be taken to produce the best effect. This new field of study is called *chronotherapy.* On the basis of its findings, new drug formulations have been devised to provide the highest levels of the active ingredient when they are most needed. One form of the bronchodilator theophylline, for example, is designed to be taken at 7 P.M. and reaches the peak levels in the blood during the night while the person is asleep. Researchers have found that oral steroids should be taken at 3 P.M. in order to reach the highest levels in the blood during the night. Timing the medications properly makes them much more effective in helping control asthma. As Dr. Richard J. Martin of the National Jewish Center for Immunology and Respiratory Medicine in Denver notes, "If you control the nighttime asthma, you can change the severity of asthma."[5]

Asthma Drugs Through History

Atropine, a type of anticholinergic drug, was widely prescribed for centuries. (Atrovent is now the preferred atropine-type drug used since it has fewer side effects than atropine.) The name *atropine* comes from Atropos, one of three mythological Greek fates. She was known for severing the web of life woven and measured by her sisters, Clotho and Lachesis. Atropine got its name because it can become a deadly poison if taken in large doses.

Plants that contained atropine were first used in India and then in Europe by the seventeenth century. The leaves were smoked until "the chest, throat, and head became light, and the cough reduced."[6] The most popular plant used for asthma was *Datura stramonium,* commonly known as jimsonweed, stinkweed, and thorn apple.

The asthma drug ephedrine was actually being used four to five thousands years ago by the Chinese. The Chinese called this herbal remedy *ma huang;* it came from the plant *Ephedra* and was used as a remedy for coughs and colds. The ancient Roman historian Pliny the Elder reported that asthmatics took an *Ephedra* extract in sweet wine to ease their symptoms. Then, for a long time, ephedrine was forgotten and no longer used. It was finally rediscovered by Japanese researchers at the beginning of the twentieth century. This led to the development of Asthmatol, the first modern brochodilator.

The hormone epinephrine (adrenaline) was first discovered at the beginning of the twentieth century. In the 1920s, adrenaline was developed as a bronchodilator for asthmatics. Hospitals may still use adrenaline for emergency treatment of severe asthma episodes.

After the action of adrenaline was understood, researchers attempted to make synthetic compounds with similar properties. A useful drug of this type, known as isoprenaline or isoproterenol, was synthesized in 1940.

In 1949, cortisone (a steroid drug) was discovered. It was highly successful in treating patients with life-threatening asthma episodes. By the 1960s, however, doctors realized that its serious side effects made it unsuitable for long-term use. (In addition to the negative effects typical of other corticosteroids, long-term use of cortisone can lead to wide mood swings and even episodes of mental illness.) Since then, a greater understanding of how steroids work and the development of steroids in aerosol form (permitting the use of smaller doses that act locally) made people realize the value of steroids in treating asthma.

In the 1960s, Dr. Roger Altounyan was studying ancient Egyptian writings describing a bronchodilator and discovered a new drug, cromolyn sodium. It is made from khellin, which comes from the seeds of the Middle Eastern plant *Ammi visnana*. Khellin is a compound that relaxes the smooth muscle. Since the airways are surrounded by smooth muscle, it opens up the narrowed passageway.

Immunotherapy

People who have atopic asthma may be treated by immunotherapy, or allergy shots. Allergy shots should be taken only if avoidance of allergens proves to be impossible and all other treatments are ineffective. However, immunotherapy should rarely be used as the sole method of asthma treatment but rather in addition to other treatments.

Allergy shots involve the injection of small doses of allergens to which the person is sensitive. The injections stimulate the production of a different kind of antibodies, IgG. The doses of the allergens are very gradually increased, and more IgG antibodies are produced. Eventually there are enough IgG antibodies around to compete with the IgE forms. So inhaled pollens or other allergens are likely to be tied up by IgG "blocking antibodies" before they have a chance to react with the specific IgE antibodies that activate mast cells. Thus the body gradually becomes less sensitive to the allergens, so exposure to them will no longer provoke an allergic reaction. This takes time. Many physicians believe that immunotherapy should be continued for at least two to five years before deciding whether it is effective in treating a particular patient with asthma. If it is effective, it should be continued for a year after the patient is symptom-free.

Exercise as a Cure?

Paul Sorvino, an actor who appeared in television's *Law and Order,* among other roles, has lived with asthma since he was ten years old. At age twenty-six, Sorvino was frustrated when he experienced an asthma episode before his 1965 Broadway show debut with Chita Rivera, Robert Burr, and Herb Edelman. One day Sorvino mentioned his asthma to his costars Burr and Edelman, who regularly practiced yoga. Edelman remarked, "Oh, that can be cured," and he and Burr demonstrated yoga exercises, which Sorvino then did himself. The next morning when Sorvino woke up, aside from mild bronchitis, his breathing was completely clear.

Sorvino continued to practice yoga exercises and found that his asthma had disappeared. In 1985, he wrote a book called *How to Become a Former Asthmatic,* which outlined a program on how to become asthma-free. He explained that these exercises "teach you to fill your lungs up from the bottom, where they have the most capacity. It enables a person to begin dealing with the affliction in an organized way."

Sorvino's young son, Michael, was diagnosed with asthma when he was three. Sorvino decided to teach his son how to do these exercises instead of relying on all of the medications prescribed for his asthma. Since Michael was so young, Sorvino and his wife had to make up games to keep up Michael's interest in these exercises. For instance, Sorvino would pretend his fingers were candles and Michael had to blow them out. Other times, he would make his hands in the shape of a bird and complain that he was too weak to fly. Michael would blow air under the bird's wings, and it would fly into the imaginary horizon.

Sorvino's view of treatment met with skepticism from physicians like Dr. Talmadge E. King from the National Jewish Hospital/National Asthma Center in Denver, who warned that Sorvino's treatment should not be viewed as a cure. Dr. King stated, "Asthma is a complex disease. We believe a total program of medical, psychosocial, drug and rehabilitation therapies is required to control the disease."

Sorvino presented numerous case histories of the people he had helped over the years with his twice-daily fifteen-minute exercises, but most asthma specialists believe that exercises to strengthen lung function are only part of the treatment program.[7]

Holistic Approach

The type of treatment program described by Dr. King is actually a holistic approach to asthma. In other words, instead of concentrating solely on medications that treat the physical symptoms, asthma patients also need to pay attention to their diets, emotions, and lifestyles, which is a more well-rounded approach.

Alternative Medicine

Homeopathy is a "natural" method of treatment that is based on the idea that a remedy can cure a disease only if it can trigger the symptoms of that disease in a healthy person. A homeopathic remedy usually contains natural substances made from animal, vegetable, or mineral sources. Therefore, it is claimed, there are no side effects. The patient is given this compound with a very tiny amount of the allergen included. One study revealed that those who were given the homeopathic remedy had 33 percent fewer asthmatic symptoms than those who were given placebos (inactive substances that subjects in the study believed were active drugs). Some critics believe that the amount of allergen used is too small to benefit patients, and benefits are largely psychological. Homeopathic medicine is becoming increasingly popular, however.

Nature's Remedies

Chemists at Harvard University have synthesized a compound called ginkgolide B, which is the active ingredient in extracts from the ginkgo tree used as a natural remedy. The substance appears to work by interfering with platelet-activating factor, one of the mediator chemicals responsible for causing asthma symptoms. This may lead to treatments for asthma. Extracts of ginkgo leaves have been used in Chinese medicine for at least five thousand years and are considered "good for the heart and lungs." Today they are used widely in Asia and Europe. In the United States, they are sold as nutritional supplements and have not yet been approved for drug use.[8]

Good nutritional habits have been known to have beneficial effects on people with allergies and asthma. For instance, a study of more than twenty-six hundred people from eighteen to seventy years old found that those who ate a diet high in magnesium had better lung function and were less likely to have experienced wheezing or other asthma symptoms during the preceding year. This statistical study supported laboratory findings that magnesium relaxes smooth muscles and widens the air passages.[9] Other studies showed that eating fish can also protect against bronchitis and asthma. Fish oil has been found to have anti-inflammatory properties. In one study, fifteen people with asthma took eighteen capsules a day of either fish oil or a placebo. Those who received the fish oil showed a decrease in their breathing difficulties.[10]

Avoidance Is the Best Treatment

It is quite clear how important a role medication plays in managing asthma in a person's daily life. However, some people believe that physicians are overemphasizing the importance of asthma drugs. What they really should be doing is stressing the value of avoidance. If a cat walks into a room, a person who is allergic to cats will probably cough and wheeze. The asthmatic's body is telling him or her to either leave the room or get rid of the cat. Instead, the allergic pet owner reaches for an inhaler and takes a quick couple of puffs to relieve the symptoms. He or she may then feel fine, but what is really happening is the inflammation in the lungs is actually getting worse because the lungs are still being exposed to the allergen. Instead of helping, the treatment is actually masking the real problem.[11]

6

Prevention

Four-year-old Kathy has had asthma since she was a baby. Her mother tried to make Kathy's bedroom as dust-free as possible. She removed all rugs, curtains, and bookshelves. However, Kathy wanted to sleep with her teddy bear. Kathy still experienced wheezing at night, and her mom believed that the teddy bear was the culprit. Kathy's mom finally tried to introduce a new bear to Kathy, one that was washable. Eventually, Kathy warmed up to this new bear, and her wheezing disappeared.[1]

Seventy-year-old Merle has had asthma much of his life. He had been hospitalized frequently and treated for severe episodes caused by pollen. Allergy shots did not help. He believed it was hopeless until about twenty years ago. That was when Merle and his wife built a new house and had an air purifier installed. This device was nothing short of a miracle. Although Merle still had some seasonal allergies, he was finally able to control his asthma with aerosols. The air filtration system actually saved him money in the long run by keeping him out of the emergency room.[2]

Unfortunately, it is not possible to prevent asthma from developing in people who inherit hypersensitive airways. But finding ways to prevent an asthma episode from coming on can make all the difference in an asthmatic's life. As we mentioned in Chapter 5, several types of asthma drugs can help prevent an episode before it happens, but avoiding asthma triggers is actually the best form of prevention. In addition, there are also devices that can be used to clear the air of foreign particles that can effect an asthmatic's lungs.

House Dust Mites

Parents of children with asthma need to focus on the elimination of the child's asthma triggers. Probably the hardest allergen to get rid of is house dust. If you look in a child's room, you will probably see loads of dust collectors—carpets, bookshelves, curtains, stuffed toys. Not only should these items be taken out of the child's room, but the room should be cleaned at least twice a week to keep the house dust from accumulating. Mattresses and pillows are also dust collectors. Hypoallergenic plastic or allergen-impermeable membrane covers will protect the child with asthma from troublesome dust allergens.

Actually, it is not only the dust itself that is the problem. House dust is a combination of everything imaginable, including fibers from bed linens, flakes of dead skin, pollen grains, pet hair, mold spores, and little pieces of insects or other bugs. One of the main dust ingredients that can trigger an asthma episode is the microscopic feces of tiny creatures called dust mites. Mites actually are not insects; like spiders, they have eight legs and belong to the group of arachnids. Dust mites thrive on house dust, eating the bits of organic matter it contains. They are too small to see without a microscope but are very numerous—up to eighteen hundred per gram of dust! Their favorite places to hide are in carpets, mattresses, feather pillows, and stuffed toys. The mite feces are so small and light that they can easily float through the air with the slightest breeze and enter a person's nasal passages—which can lead to asthma symptoms. Wet-mopping or vacuuming can remove dust from household surfaces. A vacuum cleaner equipped with special filters should be used; the exhausts of some vacuum cleaners blow the dust back into the air.

Molds

Molds are triggers that are present in the air all year round. They breed quickly in any damp environment, especially in bathrooms. In the summertime, mold can grow in mattresses and pillows if you perspire while you sleep. Molds reproduce by forming huge numbers of tiny seedlike particles called spores. Like plant pollens, mold spores are very light and drift through the air with ease and often provoke allergic reactions.

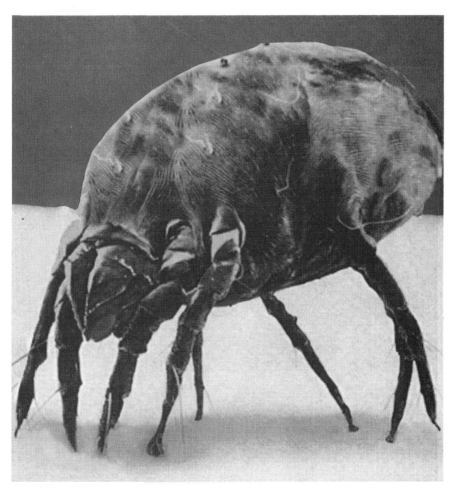

The feces of dust mites, one of the main components of dust, may trigger asthma episodes in some people. A dust mite is shown here greatly magnified.

Chlorine is a very effective mold killer. As with house dust, you can protect your mattresses and pillows from molds by putting on protective covers made of allergen-impermeable membrane. (Plastic covers can also provide protection, but many people find them uncomfortable to lie on.)

Colds and Flu

Colds and other viral infections are common triggers of asthma episodes, especially among children. It is important for people with asthma to try to avoid anyone who may have a cold. Doctors often recommend getting flu shots, but not everyone should take this advice. In fact, people who are allergic to eggs should never get a flu shot. The flu vaccine is grown on eggs and can cause a serious reaction in an egg-sensitive asthma patient. It could even be fatal.

Pets

Pets can be serious asthma triggers. Giving up a pet can be very difficult and heart-wrenching for asthma patients. People usually do not want to give up a pet, even if it causes them a severe reaction. Some people are so sensitive that the animal could be in another room and the person with asthma could still experience a reaction. The problem with pets is that their dander is usually throughout the house. Removing the pet and then cleaning the house thoroughly is the best medicine for an asthma patient.

Food Allergies

Food allergy is another trigger for some asthma patients. The obvious thing to do is to eliminate the specific food from the diet. However, there is a way to bring a favorite (but trouble-causing) food back into the diet without experiencing any reaction. It is called the elimination diet. The purpose of this is to cleanse the body of that specific food by not eating it for a while. Then, the allergic person tries eating small amounts of it. If no symptoms result, the amount can be gradually increased so that eventually the person might be able to eat a normal portion of a food that once provoked asthma episodes. However, this program should be conducted under observation by an allergist. Also, not all foods will respond to an elimination diet.

Air Pollution

Air pollution is a powerful trigger and is almost impossible to avoid in our modern world. Soot particles and chemical pollutants are produced mainly in cities and industrial areas, but they are carried all over the world by the atmosphere. Various pollution triggers for people with asthma include fog, sulfuric smoke coming from factories, ozone, cigarette smoke, perfumes, solvents, and many more. The best thing to do to avoid the outdoor pollution is to close all windows and turn on the air conditioner. Most people think of an air conditioner as a helpful device that cools and dehumidifies the air on hot summer days. An air conditioner also helps filter out pollen

The smoke coming from these factory smokestacks contains soot particles and chemical pollutants that may be dangerous to people with asthma.

grains, dust, and other foreign particles. Special air cleaning machines equipped with a HEPA filter (high-efficiency particulate air filter) may also be used to remove irritating particles from the air. People with asthma should also try to stay away from cigarette smoke at all times. Those who are sensitive to strong perfumes should avoid using scents or spending time with people who use them. Other indoor pollutants like household cleaners or toilet paper with strong odors can be replaced with scent-free brands without added perfume.

Pollen

Most asthma patients over six years old have pollen allergies. Pollen is produced by flowering plants. It contains the male sex cells and must be delivered to the female flower parts in order to form seeds. Plants that produce large, brightly colored flowers actually are not the main problem. Their pollen is usually transferred from flower to flower by insects, birds, or bats. Grasses, many trees, and other plants such as ragweed produce huge amounts of very light pollen that is spread by the wind. Pollen dust typically rises to the sky in the morning as the sun warms the air and falls to the ground in the evening as the air grows cooler. Doctors recommend that asthma patients should stay inside with the windows closed as much as possible and make sure the air conditioner is turned on. The best time to open up the windows is around midday. If people with asthma do have to leave the house, they should travel in a car with air conditioning. They should also keep their asthma

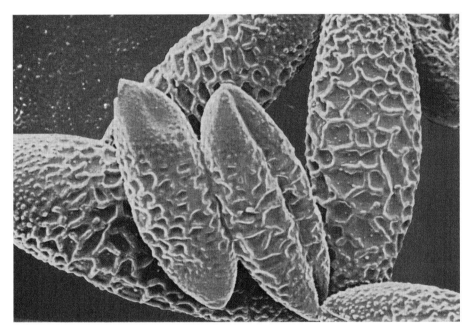

Many people are allergic to the pollen of certain plants, including the lily pollen shown here, magnified greatly.

medication handy at all times. Washing one's hair after getting home in the evening is a good routine for anyone with asthma, to remove any pollen that might have gotten in the hair while the person was outside. For similar reasons, clothes and bed coverings should be dried in a clothes dryer rather than on a line outdoors where they can pick up pollen from the air.

Exercise

Although exercise is a very common trigger among asthma patients, it should not be avoided but rather managed. Exercise is very important because it has many physical and psychological benefits. Exercise helps the heart and cardiovascular system deliver more oxygen throughout the entire body. A person whose body is physically fit will be more capable of handling an asthma episode. Exercise can also strengthen muscles and prevent muscle weakness that may be caused by certain asthma drugs. In addition, regular exercise can help reduce airway obstruction by increasing the mucus production, which can lessen the frequency of asthma episodes. Exercise can improve an asthmatic's mental attitude, too. Keeping fit will help develop positive self-esteem, a good self-image, and an optimistic outlook, which is important since many asthmatics equate exercise with having an episode.

People with asthma like to participate in such sports as jogging, dancing, cycling, weightlifting (light weights), and swimming. Doctors often recommend swimming because the air is usually warm and moist, which decreases the likeliness of an asthma episode. The best exercise is one that the person enjoys and will continue.

Olympic athletes with asthma often recommend doing warm-ups before exercising. This allows their muscles to warm up gradually before they have to endure the stress of exercise. Asthma medication should also be taken before exercising to prevent an asthma episode. However, all exercise programs should be monitored by a doctor.

Breathing Exercises

Breathing exercises can be a valuable tool for asthmatics. By doing these exercises regularly, they can strengthen the lungs, which makes it easier to improve and control asthma. Breathing exercises are also very effective for helping a person relax. There are three types of breathing exercises that asthmatics need to practice: purse-lip breathing, diaphragmatic breathing, and advanced diaphragmatic breathing.

In purse-lip breathing, one inhales through the nose, then purses the lips as if blowing out a candle, and exhales through the mouth slowly. The exhaling should be longer than the inhaling. During exhaling the person counts. As breathing becomes more efficient, he or she will be able to increase the total count for each breath.

In diaphragmatic breathing, first one breathes deeply through the nose. Putting one hand on the stomach and the other hand on the chest can help to check on whether the exercise is being done correctly. If the hand on the chest is moving while the one on the stomach is not, then the person is not breathing from the diaphragm. The stomach should rise during each inhalation, while the chest remains still. Exhaling is done similarly to the purse-lip breathing method.

Once a person has mastered normal diaphragmatic breathing, he or she can try advanced diaphragmatic breathing. With this exercise, instead of expanding the abdomen, one expands the lower ribs. This will make breathing even more efficient, will expand the lower chest, and is good for the tone of the diaphragm. This method of breathing is similar to normal diaphragmatic breathing, but the hands must be placed on the sides of the lower ribs (near the top of the abdomen). The person tries to keep the chest and abdomen from moving while breathing so that he or she can feel the sides expand.

These breathing exercises improve lung capacity, strengthen the diaphragm, help one relax, and give a person with asthma the ability to become involved in a greater variety of activities. When the proper breathing techniques are used along with daily exercises, the body will be healthy enough to fight off future asthma episodes more effectively.

7

Asthma and Society

Eight-year-old Elysa Masone has found herself caught in the middle of a court custody battle between her father, Steven Masone, and her mother, Susan Tanner. Steven wants custody of his daughter because he believes Susan is harming her. It is not the usual child abuse that is often the basis of child custody suits. Steven is worried about Elysa's health because Susan smokes and Elysa has asthma. When Elysa was three, Steven even got a court order prohibiting Susan from smoking around his daughter. That did not work. Susan still continued to smoke in Elysa's presence. Finally, Elysa had an asthma episode, and the doctor said that next time she might end up in the emergency room. Steven was afraid for his daughter so they went back to court. The judge ruled that Susan was endangering her daughter's health and gave temporary custody to Steven's mother.

Susan does not understand how she can be losing her daughter for something that is perfectly legal. In an increasing number of other cases, however, judges have been prohibiting parents from smoking around their children. According to *Legal Times,* at least eleven states have been involved with this problem, and almost all cases were decided in favor of the nonsmoker.[1]

Efforts Toward a Smoke-free Environment

Effects of cigarette smoking have gained a lot of attention in recent years. Antismoking groups have rallied to get the word out to lawmakers, begging for their right to breathe. Their efforts have not been in vain. A growing number of public places, such as restaurants, business offices, shopping malls, and airline flights, are now smoke-free.

What's in a Cigarette?

Nonsmokers have a reason to fear cigarette smoke. According to the American Lung Association, tobacco smoke contains about four thousand chemicals, including two hundred known toxins, such as benzene, formaldehyde, and carbon monoxide. When a cigarette smoker takes a puff, these chemicals are released into the air. Not only does the smoker inhale these toxins, but everyone around that person does, too.[2]

The effect of cigarette smoking
on the lungs

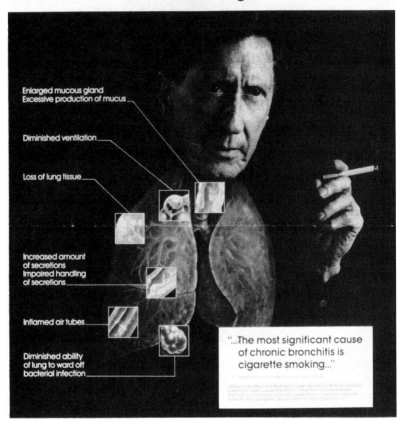

Enlarged mucous gland
Excessive production of mucus

Diminished ventilation

Loss of lung tissue

Increased amount
of secretions
Impaired handling
of secretions

Inflamed air tubes

Diminished ability
of lung to ward off
bacterial infection

"...The most significant cause
of chronic bronchitis is
cigarette smoking..."

The carbon monoxide from cigarette smoke can be very dangerous. Many smokers develop illnesses such as bronchitis, emphysema, and lung cancer.

What Does Cigarette Smoking Do to the Lungs?

When cigarette smoke is inhaled, the chemicals, such as carbon monoxide, go directly into the lungs. Carbon monoxide is a particularly dangerous component of cigarette smoke. Once it is absorbed into the bloodstream, it combines with hemoglobin, a substance in the red blood cells that carries oxygen to all the vital organs in the body. The carbon monoxide in the blood keeps the oxygen from reaching the brain, heart, lungs, and other organs. Cigarette smoke also damages the cilia in the lining of the airways; eventually they become unable to sweep the mucus and foreign particles out of the lungs and up toward the throat. Some pollutants in cigarette smoke remain in the lungs. As a result, a person can develop illnesses like bronchitis, emphysema, or lung cancer. Some smokers complain about a "smoker's cough," which can be an obvious sign of serious damage to the lungs. Thus, smoking can really be hard on a normal person's body—can you imagine what it can do to someone with asthma?[3]

Secondhand Smoke Is Linked to Asthma

If smokers want to contaminate their own lungs, it is their choice, but when they are smoking around another person, they take away the decision from the other person. Smoking can be hazardous in its own right, but it can be even more serious for people who receive secondhand smoke, especially for those with asthma. Recent studies have confirmed that there is connection between secondhand smoke and developing asthma. One study published in the *New England Journal of Medicine* focused on the relationship between the amount of exposure to secondhand smoke and the frequency of asthma episodes as compared to the preceding year. It was reported that children exposed to the most secondhand smoke had 70 percent more asthma episodes than those who had little or no exposure.[4]

The Centers for Disease Control and Prevention (CDC) in Atlanta estimates that mothers who smoke ten or more cigarettes a day actually cause as many as twenty-six thousand new cases of asthma each year.[5]

Common Pollutants in Our Environment

Cigarette smoke is only one of a number of pollutants that affect the quality of our air. The Environmental Protection Agency (EPA) has been designated to test the most common pollutants in the environment so that their levels are below the maximum values set by the Clean Air Act. The Clean Air Act is designed to improve the environment by placing stricter regulations on the release of these pollutants that are literally poisoning the air we breathe.

Carbon monoxide is a very common toxin. It is emitted from vehicles. If it is inhaled, it can reduce the blood's ability to carry oxygen to the body's organs and tissues. Stricter emissions tests during vehicle inspections have lessened the level of this poisonous gas. The level of carbon monoxide fell 34 percent in the past decade.

Lead is a pollutant that can be found in our water and food, or lead particles can be inhaled from the air. Lead can

If inhaled, the carbon monoxide from these vehicles can reduce the blood's ability to carry oxygen to the body's organs and tissues.

lead to neurological problems, mental retardation, or other disorders. Lead-free gasoline has helped a great deal in lowering the lead levels in the environment. The level of lead fell 89 percent in the past decade.

Nitrogen dioxide is formed when fuel is burned at high temperatures. It is produced in the manufacture of fertilizer and explosives. It also gives cigarette smoke its yellow-brown tinge. It can irritate the lungs and cause respiratory problems. Better fuel efficiency has reduced nitrogen dioxide emissions. The level of nitrogen dioxide fell 8 percent in the past decade.

Ozone pollution is better known as smog. Smog is created when nitrogen oxide and other compounds emitted from cars and industrial plants are combined and then exposed to sunlight. The ozone in smog should not be confused with the ozone layer in the upper atmosphere (which protects us from the sun's harmful UV rays). Smog can damage biological tissues and cells. It is higher in the afternoon on hot summer days; people with asthma should try to stay indoors in air-conditioned rooms at the peak ozone hours. The level of ozone fell 21 percent in the past decade.

Particulate matter includes dust, soot, and smoke, which can damage the lungs and the airways and can also help cause cancer. The level of particulates fell 17 percent in the past decade.

Sulfur dioxide is common in cities where energy is produced by burning fossil fuels, such as coal. Sulfur dioxide is damaging to the respiratory system and can contribute to heart disease. The level of sulfur dioxide fell 23 percent in the past decade.[6]

Why Are Asthma Rates Still Rising?

Everyone agrees that air pollution is a major trigger for asthma episodes. Yet over the past decade, while we have been making impressive strides in improving air quality, the numbers of asthma cases and asthma-related deaths have continued to increase. What is wrong?

Several explanations have been suggested for the rising asthma rates. The energy crisis of the mid-1970s resulted in a greater emphasis on conserving oil and other fuels. New buildings were designed and older ones were remodeled with extra insulation and more tightly sealed joints to reduce heat loss in the winter and make summer air conditioning more efficient. The tighter construction means that indoor air pollutants cannot leak out, either. They build up in the air, increasing the exposure of people who live or work in the buildings. Moreover, there has been an increase in the use of carpeting and soft furnishings, which collect dust and (in the case of synthetic fabrics) may also release small amounts of irritating chemcials into the air.[7]

Some doctors believe that the wide availability of over-the-counter beta-agonist inhalers, such as Primatene Mist®, may not be an entirely good thing. Many people tend to rely on them too much, instead of consulting a doctor and getting proper treatment including anti-inflammatory drugs. A statistical study of asthma deaths in New Zealand at first appeared to support this view. An epidemic of asthma deaths suddenly began there in 1976. In 1981, it was suggested that beta-agonist drugs might be involved in the sudden increase in the asthma death rate. This theory received wide publicity, and after that, the death rate fell somewhat. But a group of researchers noticed that 1976, when the epidemic began, was also the year that a particular bega-agonist drug, fenoterol, was introduced in New Zealand. (This particlar drug was never approved for use in the United States.) The researchers ran a detailed study of fenoterol users, compared to asthma patients who used other treatments, and reported in 1989 that this one drug was actually the cause of the extra deaths. People who used other inhaled beta agonists did not have an increased death rate. On the basis of the study, New Zealand authorities stopped the sale of fenoterol. Immediately there was a dramatic drop in the asthma death rate![8]

Many researchers believe that socioeconomic factors play an important role in asthma deaths. In the United States, the death rates are highest among African Americans and Hispanics. These are precisely the population groups most likely to live in poor city neighborhoods, in overcrowded conditions that can lower indoor air quality and promote respiratory illness. People in these groups also receive less regular medical care than the rest of the population—and thus they are less likely to receive the proper medical treatment for asthma.[9]

Air Pollution Exceeds Safe Limits

We have made great strides in reducing the harmful pollutants in the environment over the past decade. Even so, according to American Lung Association estimates, 66 percent of Americans live in areas that exceed federal limits for carbon monoxide, ozone, lead, and other major pollutants.[10] Our hard-won gains may not be safe. Many influential people in the government now believe that strict air quality standards place too great a burden on industry. "Unfortunately, while the lung association continues to fight for strict clean air standards to protect Americans' health, Congress is attempting to weaken or even destroy those protections," remarked Irwin M. Berlin, a member of the American Lung Association.[11]

Some of the new proposals make sense, allowing companies to work out the best solutions for their own conditions rather than having to follow precisely spelled-out guidelines that may add expense without really helping air quality. If we relax air pollution standards too far, though, we may find ourselves back in the "bad old days," when weather conditions and pollution sometimes combined to produce epidemics of respiratory illness and death. In 1948, for example, heavy concentrations of smog caused the deaths of twenty people, and six thousand people became ill in Donora, Pennsylvania. In December 1952, a thick blanket of smog covered London, which sent out emergency smog alerts. Tests of air samples showed that levels of sulfur dioxide and particulates had increased tenfold. The smog caused the deaths of four thousand people. Studies have shown that 88 percent of asthmatics have respiratory problems when air pollution levels increase.[12]

8

Asthma and the Future

Nancy Sander founded Mothers of Asthmatics, a nonprofit educational and support group, after her daughter Brooke came close to death during an asthma episode when she was seven years old. The episode occurred in school, and no one there knew enough about the disease to realize it was a medical emergency. Desperate to understand this frightening illness, Nancy tried to dig up as much information as she could on asthma so she could help Brooke manage this disease and live a normal life. By educating herself, Nancy was able to show her daughter what signs to look for, what questions to ask, and what treatment to pursue. With some knowledge and a good management plan, Nancy and Brooke were able to work together and bring the asthma under control.[1]

Asthma Support Groups

After Nancy Sander was able to help her daughter take back control of her life, she realized she could help others do the same. Support groups for asthmatics and their families are becoming a growing trend. These asthma groups are designed to educate asthmatics and their families. They learn the basics of asthma and try to gain an understanding of what is involved. They discuss their symptoms, triggers, ways of coping with the disease, and even different types of medications available. They also touch on the emotional aspects of the disease, such as the effects it has on the family, relationships with other children at school, and their reluctance to participate in extracurricular activities. Support groups are also designed to help with the child's self-esteem.

In addition to the local support groups that meet face-to-face and keep in touch by phone, there are groups that connect only by way of computers and modems. A number of Internet newsgroups and web sites provide asthma information and opportunities to share questions and concerns with others facing the same problems.

Asthma Summer Camps

Special summer camps provide recreation and sports for children with asthma in relaxed, protected surroundings. The children learn to get involved in activities without worrying about the reactions of other people who do not understand their disease; they do not feel embarrassed about their medical problems since all of the other kids also have asthma. The

103

camps are also equipped with a medical staff in case anybody has an asthma episode.

Learn From Puppets

The American Lung Association has created a program that introduces a different approach to educating the public about asthma. This program is called "Kids on the Block" and uses puppets to teach children all about various diseases and disabilities. The puppets portray children with diseases and give other children a better idea of what it is all about.[2]

National Guidelines of Asthma Management

Education is very important in asthma management. In fact, an organization called Asthma Zero Mortality Coalition (AZMC) believes that people in the United States do not understand the seriousness of asthma and how to manage and control this common illness. They believe that this lack of awareness is responsible for the increasing mortality rate among asthmatics. Therefore, their objective is to inform the public through an educational campaign. Their goal is to dramatically reduce the asthma deaths by the year 2000.[3]

Education is so necessary that it is also one of the national guidelines of asthma management devised by members of the National Heart, Lung, and Blood Institute through its National Asthma Education Program. The other guidelines include a proper diagnosis using objective measures such as lung function tests, appropriate and effective medication, and reduction and avoidance of asthma triggers.[4]

Searching for an Asthma Gene

Although asthma management is a vital part of asthma treatment, researchers are continuing to search for an asthma gene. It has been known for years that people inherit a tendency to develop asthma, but the discovery of an asthma gene could be the key to finding a cure.

For years, scientists have suspected that the asthma gene was one of thousands on the 11th pair of chromosomes. In 1992, a team of researchers at Oxford University in London had narrowed the possibilities down to one of one hundred genes on chromosome 11. In 1994, they established that the gene forms the receptor on mast cells, to which immunoglobulin E binds. People with a particular variant of this gene were likely to have high levels of IgE in their blood and thus would tend to overreact to allergens. (Oddly enough, the gene seems to cause trouble only when it is inherited from the mother.) The scientists are cautious about the findings since the connection was observed in only a small number of families. "I think they might have at least a partial answer and it could be very important," said Marshall Plaut, chief of the asthma and allergy branch of the National Institute of Allergy and Infectious Diseases.[5] This gene may help researchers find genes that play a role in asthma in other people. The identification of an IgE receptor gene also points the way to new treatments—once the structure of the receptor is known, biochemists can design drugs to attach to it, preventing IgE from binding to the mast cells.[6]

Some researchers theorize that asthma may involve more

than one gene, and in 1995, another research group reported the discovery of a different gene on chromosome 11 that produces a protein that is found in cells in the airway lining. This protein has anti-inflammatory effects and helps regulate the immune system—so it is actually an antiasthma gene rather than as asthma gene. (A defective version of the gene might thus result in susceptibility to asthma.)[7] It appears that chromosome 11 is only part of the asthma story, however. In 1994, a study of families of asthma patients found evidence that a gene on chromosome 5 regulates IgE levels in the blood. People who inherit a particular version of this gene have high IgE levels and thus are more likely to develop allergic reactions and asthma.[8]

More Clues From Basic Research

In a recent study, researchers at Johns Hopkins University have isolated a protein that plays a role in a serious type of allergic reaction. The protein, called histamine-releasing factor (HRF), is one of a large collection of proteins that cause about 18 percent of the population to have severe, long-lasting allergic reactions. Exposure to an allergen actually produces a double reaction: an immediate reaction and then another one, hours later. Half of the people with late-phase reactions develop asthma, chronic sniffles, and other persistent symptoms.

Researchers hope to use a test for HRF to identify people likely to have late-phase reactions. If they can identify the cell receptors to which HRF must attach to produce its effects, they can also develop drugs to block the reaction. But the reaction is a very complex one, notes Dr. Susan M. MacDonald, one of the Johns Hopkins researchers, and the whole group of proteins will have to be identified before these severe allergic reactions can be fully understood and controlled.[9]

Another Johns Hopkins research group has been concentrating on bronchospasm. According to Dr. Alkis Togias, the leader of the group, muscles in the airway walls contract in response to irritants, both in people with asthma and in people with normal lungs. The key difference lies in what happens after that. Normal people react to the reduced air flow by breathing deeply, relaxing and stretching the airway muscles and opening up the air passages. The airway muscles of people with asthma do not relax after the bronchospasm, and the researchers are trying to find out why. In one study, both asthmatics and nonasthmatics were given the drug methacholine to inhale. This drug is an irritant that provokes breathing problems in people with asthma. The nonasthmatics were then told not to breathe deeply during the test, to see what would happen. "The nonasthmatics suddenly began to have breathing difficulties remarkably similar to those of asthmatics," says Dr. Togias. The researcher, who was also one of the normal volunteers in the study, says that the experience gave him new insight into what his patients go through. "When you can't breathe, no matter how you try, you understand the feelings of anxiety and distress of asthmatics. It certainly gives you more empathy with patients."[10]

Other studies have found that the helper T cells may play an important role in asthma. When these cells are triggered, they produce a group of "messenger" proteins called cytokines

107

that set off a reaction that causes the airways to constrict. In a double-blind study, subjects were given a drug called cyclosporin, which prevents the process that activates helper T cells. The study revealed that this drug improved the patients' breathing and reduced the number of severe asthma episodes. However, cyclosporin is not a miracle drug to use in the future. It can have serious side effects. Instead, researchers are concentrating on using monoclonal antibodies, very specific antibodies specially made to block the helper T cells.[11]

Other studies of the mediator chemicals involved in allergic reactions are already yielding promising new drugs. At the 1995 International Conference of the American Academy of Allergy & Immunology, researchers reported on clinical trials of two drugs, both aimed at mediators called leukotrienes. Leukotrienes have been found to produce typical asthma symptoms, and they are released by lung cells during asthma episodes. Drug researchers at Abbott Laboratories and Zeneca Pharmaceuticals have been attempting to short-circuit the asthmatic reaction by devising drugs to interfere with leukotriene action. The Abbott drug, zileuton, blocks leukotriene production, and the Zeneca drug, zafirlukast, ties up the leukotriene receptors and prevents them from acting on the airway cells. Tests on nearly eight hundred asthma patients revealed that both drugs improve asthma symptoms.[12]

Soon these and other new drugs will be available to help in asthma management. With effective treatments and a stepped-up educational program to increase public awareness, we may ultimately come very close to the goal of zero asthma deaths.

Q & A

Q. A boy in my class has asthma and coughs a lot. Can I catch asthma from him?

A. No. Asthma is not a contagious disease. There are no "asthma germs" that can be transmitted from one person to another.

Q. My little sister has asthma. Will she outgrow it?

A. Probably not. Some cases of asthma in young children get better or disappear by the time they are teenagers. However, the asthma may return in later life.

Q. If I marry somebody with asthma, will my children have it too?

A. Perhaps, but not necessarily. Asthma is hereditary, but scientists believe there are a number of genes involved. So the children of someone with asthma are not sure to develop it but have a better than average chance of having asthma.

Q. What should I do if someone in school has an asthma episode?

A. If someone suddenly begins coughing, wheezing, and having difficulty breathing, contact a nurse or doctor as quickly as possible. Try to stay calm—emotional reactions can make an asthma episode worse. A person who has had asthma episodes before may wear an ID bracelet or carry a card listing what medications to take during an episode.

Q. Taking drugs every time I feel an episode coming on seems kind of wimpy. Can't I train my lungs to get stronger if I try to "tough it out?"

A. No. A mild episode might go away by itself, but it might get worse instead. If you let it go too far, you could wind up in the hospital. If you don't keep up with the proper treatment plan, your lungs may get more and more damaged. Using a peak flow meter to monitor your lung function can help you tell when you need to take the medications to stop episodes before they go too far.

Q. A lot of my friends smoke. Would it really matter if I smoke a cigarette now and then?

A. Smoking is not a smart thing for anybody to do, and it's a particularly bad choice for someone with asthma. Cigarette smoke damages the airways and the lungs and makes the problem even worse.

Q. Okay, no cigarettes. What about pot?

A. Marijuana can be even more harmful to your lungs than regular cigarettes—and it's illegal, besides. Marijuana leaves may also contain Aspergillus molds, which can cause permanent damage to your lungs.

Q. I took beclomethasone when I was having an episode, and it didn't help. I thought it was supposed to be such a great asthma drug. What happened?

A. Some drugs, such as bronchodilators, are good for stopping asthma episodes once they have started. Inhaled corticosteroids such as beclomethasone work differently. They *prevent* episodes. But they usually have to be taken for a few weeks to become effective; and you have to continue taking them every day for them to continue working.

Q. I went out for the cross-country team this year, but in my third race I suddenly couldn't breathe and had to stop. The same thing happened the next week. Do I have to give up running?

A. You appear to have exercise-induced asthma, but that doesn't mean you can't continue running. You just have to be careful to warm up thoroughly before a race. Your doctor may also prescribe an inhaled drug for you to take before you run. Don't give up. People with asthma have won Olympic gold medals!

Q. If I get asthma episodes, does that mean I have allergies?

A. Very likely. But air pollution and other things can also be asthma triggers without causing an actual allergy.

Asthma Timeline

4000 B.C.—The Chinese used ma huang (ephedrine) as an asthma remedy.

400 B.C.—Hippocrates used the term asthma to describe wheezing.

200 B.C.—Galen described clinical signs of asthma and recommended exposure to volcanic gases as a treatment.

A.D. 600—Paulus Aegineta used drugs to get rid of excess mucus.

1100s—Maimonides suggested that asthma is hereditary.

1500s—Jerome Cardan noted an environmental link and cured King Edward VI of asthma.

1698—Sir John Floyer described contraction of bronchial muscles.

1794—Dr. William Cullen complained about difficulties of diagnosis.

1800s—Aerosols were used to treat asthma.

1900—Japanese researchers rediscovered ephedrine.

1920s—Adrenaline was first used as a bronchodilator for asthma.

1939—National Home for Jewish Children started asthma treatment program.

1940s—Dr. C. Murray Peshkin treated allergy by "parentectomy."

1949—Cortisone was discovered.

1951—Dr. Allan Hurst reported that changes in the immune system occur during an asthma episode.

1960s—Dr. Roger Altounyan discovered cromolyn sodium.

1966—Kimishige and Teruko Ishizaka discovered immunoglobulin E (IgE).

1960s—Dr. Irving Itkin reported on the role of hyperreactive airways.

1970s—Common triggers of asthma (allergens and others) were identified.

1991—NIH guidelines stressed the importance of controlling inflammation.

For More Information

ALLERGY-FREE
1502 Pine Dr.
Dickinson, TX 77539
1-800-ALLERGY (free color catalog and information)

Cooperates with physicians in monitoring patient compliance and offers discounts on products through Preferred Physician Pricing Program.

American Academy of Allergy and Immunology
611 E. Well St.
Milwaukee, WI 53202
1-800-822-2762 (24-hour hotline)

Pamphlets, referrals to local allergists; in conjunction with GlaxoWellcome, offers free Personal Asthma Management Monitor.

American Lung Association
1740 Broadway
New York, NY 10019

Pamphlets, programs, and local support groups.

Allergy and Asthma Network/Mothers of Asthmatics
3554 Chain Bridge Rd. #200
Fairfax, VA 22030
1-800-878-4403

Resource list, general information, and monthly newsletter, *The MA Report.*

Asthma and Allergy Foundation of America
1125 15th St. NW, #502
Washington, DC 20005
1-800-727-8462

Books, pamphlets, bimonthly newsletter, *Advance,* referrals to support groups, and training classes in asthma management.

National Asthma Education and Prevention Program of the National Heart, Lung, and Blood Institute
P.O. Box 30105
Bethesda, MD 20824
1-301-251-1222

Pamphlets, reprints, and twice-yearly newsletter, *Asthma Memo.*

National Jewish Center for Immunology and Respiratory Medicine
1400 Jackson St.
Denver, CO 80206
1-800-552-5864 (24-hour Med Facts information hotline)

Booklets, information packets; nurses answer questions about asthma; COPE Program offers testing, evaluation, education, and treatment plans.

Chapter Notes

Chapter 1

1. M. Eric Gershwin and E. L. Klingelhofer, *Asthma: Stop Suffering, Start Living* (Reading, Mass.: Addison-Wesley, 1992), p. 20.

Chapter 2

1. "Is It All Greek To You?" *Current Health 2,* October 1993, p. 11.

2. Ibid.; John Carpi, "Asthma Strategies: Huffing and Puffing," *Medical World News,* September 1992, p. 19.

3. Francois Haas and Sheila Sperber Haas, *The Essential Asthma Book* (New York: Scribner's, 1987), p. 88.

4. Carpi, p. 20.

5. Howard G. Rapaport and Shirley Motter Linde, *The Complete Allergy Guide* (New York: Simon & Schuster, 1970), p. 119.

6. Haas, p. 70.

7. Carpi, p. 20.

8. Mary Ann Fitzharris, *A Place to Heal: The History of National Jewish Center for Immunology and Respiratory Medicine* (Denver: National Jewish, 1989), p. 68.

9. Ibid., p. 96.

10. Ibid., p. 97.

11. Claude Lenfant and Nikolai Khaltaev, eds., *Global Strategy for Asthma Management and Prevention: NHLBI/WHO Workshop Report* (Bethesda, Md.: National Institutes of Health, 1993), pp. xiii-xiv.

Chapter 3

1. "Jackie Joyner-Kersee: Fighting Asthma," *Pharmacy Times,* June 1993, p. 33.

2. Francois Haas and Sheila Sperber Haas, *The Essential Asthma Book* (New York: Scribner's, 1987), p. 9.

3. Felice J. Freyer, "Controlling Asthma in Children," *Star-Ledger* (Newark, N.J.), June 4, 1995, sec. 6, pp. 1-2.

4. Nathaniel Altman, *What You Can Do About Asthma* (New York: Dell, 1991), p. 87.

5. Ibid., p. 28.

6. Geri Harrington, *The Asthma Self-Care Book* (New York: HarperPerennial, 1991), pp. 199-201.

7. Nancy Sander, *A Parent's Guide to Asthma* (New York: Penguin, 1994), p. 102.

Chapter 4

1. Christine Gorman, "Asthma: The Hidden Killer," *Time,* August 7, 1995, p. 56.

2. "Accepting a New Diagnosis," *New Directions,* Spring 1993, p. 2.

3. K. M. Reese, "A Spurious Case of Asthma," *Chemical & Engineering News,* March 4, 1996, p. 56.

4. Claude Lenfant and Nikolai Khaltaev, eds., *Global Strategy for Asthma Management and Prevention: NHLBI/WHO Workshop Report* (Bethesda, Md.: National Institutes of Health, 1993), p. 49; James L. Bennington, ed., *Saunders Dictionary & Encyclopedia of Laboratory Medicine and Technology* (Philadelphia: Saunders, 1984), pp. 1414-1415.

5. Francois Haas and Sheila Sperber Haas, *The Essential Asthma Book* (New York: Scribner's, 1987), p. 80.

6. Nancy Sander, *A Parent's Guide to Asthma* (New York: Penguin, 1994), p. 103.

7. Yoshihiro Kikuchi, et al., "Chemosensitivity and Perception of Dyspnea in Patients with a History of Near-Fatal Asthma," *New England Journal of Medicine,* May 12, 1994, p. 1329; Peter J. Barnes, "Blunted Perception and Death from Asthma" (editorial), *New England Journal of Medicine,* May 12, 1994, p. 1383.

8. Arthur J. Torre, contributions to a workshop of the Under Sea Hyperbaric Medical Society, June 1995.

9. Ibid.

10. Ibid.

Chapter 5

1. John Carpi, "Asthma Strategies: Huffing and Puffing," *Medical World News,* September 1992, p. 19.

2. Geri Harrington, *The Asthma Self-Care Book* (New York: HarperPerennial, 1991), pp. 75-77.

3. Claude Lenfant and Nikolai Khaltaev, eds., *Global Strategy for Asthma Management and Prevention: NHLBI/WHO Workshop Report* (Bethesda, Md.: National Institutes of Health, 1993), p. 78; Arthur J. Torre, personal communication.

4. Arthur J. Torre, contributions to a workshop of the Under Sea Hyperbaric Medical Society, June 1995.

5. Susan Gilbert, "New Drugs Are Precisely Timed To Match Body's Biological Clock," *The New York Times,* March 6, 1996, p. C10.

6. Francois Haas and Sheila Sperber Haas, *The Essential Asthma Book* (New York: Scribner's, 1987), p. 88.

7. Susan Reed, "Don't Hold Your Breath for an Asthma Cure: Paul Sorvino Says Exercise Your Lungs Instead," *People,* June 24, 1985, p. 101.

8. John Noble Wilford, "Ancient Tree Yields Secrets of Potent Healing Substance," *The New York Times,* March 1, 1988, p. C3.

9. John Britton, et. al., "Dietary Magnesium, Lung Function, Wheezing, and Airway Hyper-reactivity in a Random Adult Population Sample," *Lancet,* August 6, 1994, pp. 357-362.

10. "Breathing Easier," *Prevention,* April 1989, p. 10.

11. Christine Gorman, "Asthma: Deadly But Treatable," *Time,* June 22, 1992, pp. 61-62.

Chapter 6

1. M. Eric Gershwin and E. L. Klingelhofer, *Asthma: Stop Suffering, Start Living* (Reading, Mass.: Addison-Wesley, 1992), p. 63.

2. Ibid., p. 60.

Chapter 7

1. Andrea Sachs, "Home Smoke-Free Home," *Time,* October 25, 1993, p. 56.

2. Linda Carroll, "Second-hand Smoke Increases Bronchial Symptoms in Adults," *Medical Tribune for the Internet and Cardiologist,* December 15, 1995, p. 7.

3. M. Eric Gershwin and E. L. Klingelhofer, *Asthma: Stop Suffering, Start Living* (Reading, Mass.: Addison-Wesley, 1992), pp. 70-71.

4. "Stronger Data Link Smoking to Asthma in Young," *The New York Times,* June 15, 1993, p. C9.

5. "Asthma Update: The Newest Thinking and Treatments," *Child,* April 1994, p. 28.

6. Ken Miller, "Air Quality Improved for Millions in Past Decade," *The Courier-News* (Bridgewater, N.J.), November 3, 1993, p. A-5; "Air Pollution and Asthma: a Connection?" *Lungline Letter,* Spring 1990, p. 3.

7. A. Sonia Buist and William M. Vollmer, "Preventing Deaths from Asthma," *New England Journal of Medicine,* December 8, 1994, p. 1584.

8. Neil Pearce, et al., "End of New Zealand Asthma Mortality Epidemic," *Lancet,* January 7, 1995, pp. 41-44.

9. David M. Lang and Marcia Polansky, "Patterns of Asthma Mortality in Philadelphia from 1969 to 1991," *New England Journal of Medicine,* December 8, 1994, p. 1542.

10. "Asthma Update: The Newest Thinking and Treatments," *Child,* April 1994, p. 28.

11. Barry Carter, "A Matter of Life and Breath," *Sunday Star-Ledger* (Newark, N.J.), June 4, 1995, sec. 6, p. 1.

12. Gershwin and Klingelhofer, p. 50.

Chapter 8

1. Deborah Berger, "Asthma Doesn't Have to Stop You," *Parade,* June 16, 1991, p. 15.

2. Joan Whitlow, "Asthma: Puppets Teach Kids the Perils of Disease." *Sunday Star-Ledger* (Newark, N.J.), May 31, 1992, sec. 6, pp. 1-2.

3. "Coalition Aims to Reduce Asthma Deaths by the Year 2000," *Pharmacy Times,* November 1993, p. 21.

4. Claude Lenfant, M.D., and Robinson Fullwood, M.S.P.H., "New Directions for Asthma Management in the 1990s," *American Family Physician,* May 1992, p. 2027.

5. Associated Press, "Asthma, Hay Fever Research Hints Cause Could Be Genetic," *The Courier-News* (Bridgewater, N.J.), June 1, 1994, p. A-6.

6. "How Mothers Pass on Asthma," *New Scientist,* June 11, 1994, p. 18.

7. J. G. Hay, et al., "Human CC10 Gene Expression in an Airway Epithelium and Subchromosomal Locus Suggest Linkage to Airway Disease," *American Journal of Physiology,* April 1995, pp. L565-575.

8. D. A. Meyers, et al., "Evidence for a Locus Regulating Total Serum IgE Levels Mapping to Chromosome 5," *Genomics,* September 15, 1994, pp. 464-470.

9. Associated Press, "Newly Isolated Protein Tied to Severe Allergies," *The New York Times,* August 8, 1995, p. C7.

10. Warren E. Leary, "Study Induces Asthma Symptoms, Pointing to a Failure to Relax," *The New York Times,* November 1, 1995, p. C13.

11. Phyllida Brown, "Overactive T Cells May Cause Asthma," *New Scientist,* February 15, 1992, p. 26.

12. Katie Rogers R. Ph., "Leukotriene Inhibitors Shown to Improve Asthma Patients," *Drug Topics,* April 10, 1995, p. 27.

Glossary

acute—Brief (lasting days to weeks).

adrenergic—Having effects similar to those of the hormone adrenaline; also called beta-agonist.

airways—The bronchi and bronchioles, the tubes through which air flows in the lungs.

allergy—An acquired hypersensitivity to a foreign substance (an allergen) involving IgE antibodies.

alveoli (sing. alveolus)—The tiny air sacs in the lungs where gas exchange takes place.

anticholinergic—Blocking the mediator chemical acetylcholine.

anti-inflammatory—Blocking the reactions of inflammation.

atopic—Allergic.

bronchi (sing. bronchus)—The larger air tubes of the lungs.

bronchioles—Smaller air tubes of the lungs that branch off from the bronchi.

bronchiolitis—Inflammation of the bronchioles.

bronchitis—Inflammation of the bronchi.

bronchoconstriction—Narrowing of the bronchioles, resulting in airflow limitation.

bronchodilator—A drug that dilates (opens up) the bronchial tubes.

bronchospasm—A sudden brief contraction of the muscles in the airway walls, narrowing the air passages.

chronic—Lasting for years or possibly a lifetime.

chronotherapy—The administration of medications at the time of day or night that will produce the highest concentrations in the blood when they are most needed.

controller medications—Drugs taken daily on a long-term basis to bring and keep persistent asthma under control.

corticosteroids—Hormones of the adrenal gland that have antiallergic and anti-inflammatory effects.

dander—Scales of dead skin; dandruff.

dyspnea—Difficult breathing.

EIA—Exercise-induced asthma.

eosinophils—A type of white blood cells active during an asthma episode.

exacerbation—An aggravation or worsening of asthma; an episode.

expiration—Breathing out; exhalation.

forced expiratory volume (FEV)—The amount of air exhaled after a specific time of breathing out forcefully as fast as possible.

forced vital capacity (FVC)—The total amount of air exhaled after inhaling deeply and breathing out forcefully as fast as possible.

HEPA filter—High-efficiency particulate air filter; a device that cleans the air of particles that could irritate the airways.

hyperreactivity (hyperresponsiveness)—A tendency to react (producing symptoms) to an irritant (or an amount of an irritant) that does not bother people with normal lung function.

immunoglobulin—An antibody protein. IgE antibodies are active in allergic reactions; the defenses against disease germs involve IgG and other types of antibodies.

inhaler—A device that creates a mist of a drug that can then be drawn directly into the respiratory passages.

irritant—A substance that may cause inflammation of the airways and limitation of airflow.

maintenance medication—Drugs given on a regular basis to control asthma.

mast cell—A type of immune-system cell to which IgE antibodies can bind when sensitized by an allergen, causing the release of histamine and other inflammatory substances.

nebulizer—A device that converts liquid into a spray; a type of inhaler.

nocturnal asthma—Asthma episodes that occur at night during sleep.

peak expiratory flow (PEF) rate—The highest expiratory flow rate during a forced exhalation.

peak flow meter—A device that measures the PEF.

pulmonary function test—A test or series of tests to measure lung function and capacity.

reliever medications—Short-acting bronchodilators that relieve airflow limitation during an acute asthma episode; also called rescue medicine.

spirometer—A machine that measures various air volumes during inhalation and exhalation and graphs them against the time.

sputum—Coughed-up matter, including mucus and foreign particles.

trigger—A substance or condition (such as cold or exercise) that provokes an asthma episode.

vital capacity (VC)—The amount of air that is exhaled after inhaling deeply; about 80 percent of the total lung capacity.

wheeze—A whistling sound heard when a person breathes through narrowed airways.

Further Reading

Books

Altman, Nathaniel. *What You Can Do About Asthma.* New York: Bell, 1991.

Fitzharris, Mary Ann. *A Place to Heal: The History of National Jewish Center for Immunology and Respiratory Medicine.* Denver: National Jewish Center for Immunology and Respiratory Medicine, 1989.

Haas, Francois, and Sheila Sperber Haas. *The Essential Asthma Book.* New York: Scribner's, 1987.

Hager, Linda, and Beth W. Orenstein, eds. *Breathe Easy: Self-Help for Respiratory Ailments.* Emmaus, Pa.: Rodale Press, 1995.

Hannaway, Paul J. *The Asthma Self-Help Book: How to Live a Normal Life in Spite of Your Condition.* Rocklin, Calif.: Prima, 1992.

Harrington, Geri. *The Asthma Self-Care Book.* New York: HarperCollins, 1991.

Lenfant, Claude and Nikolai Khaltaev, eds. *Global Strategy for Asthma Management and Prevention: NHLBI/WHO Workshop Report.* Bethesda, Md.: National Heart, Lung, and Blood Institute, National Institutes of Health, January 1995.

Null, Gary. *No More Allergies.* New York: Villard, 1992.

Plaut, Thomas F. *Children with Asthma.* 2nd ed. Amherst, Mass.: Pedipress, 1988.

————. *One Minute Asthma.* Amherst, Mass.: Pedipress, Inc., 1995.

Sander, Nancy. *A Parent's Guide to Asthma.* New York: Penguin, 1994.

Articles

"A Parent's Guide to Asthma." *Rodale's Allergy Relief,* April 1989, pp. 1–2, 7–8.

Arnst, Catherine. "Trying to Knock the Wind out of Asthma." *Business Week,* June 20, 1994, pp. 184–185.

Baron-Faust, Rita. "Asthma Update: The Newest Thinking and Treatments." *Child,* April 1994, pp. 28–30.

Carpi, John. "Asthma Strategies: Huffing and Puffing." *Medical World News,* September 1992, pp. 19–23.

Gorman, Christine. "Asthma: Deadly—But Treatable." *Time,* June 22, 1992, pp. 61–62.

LeGro, Bill, and Cemela London. "Take Control of Your Asthma Now!" *Prevention,* May 1992, pp. 60–122.

Scheinholtz, Debby Friss. "Coping with Asthma." *Parents,* April 1992, pp. 118–124.

"Stop Childhood Asthma." *Prevention,* February 1993, pp. 72–75, 124–125.

"Treating Asthma: A Killer Gathers Strength." *Drug Topics,* April 8, 1991, pp. 38–48.

Wein, Bibi. "Waiting to Exhale." *Self,* June 1995, pp. 152–153.

Weinstein, Allan. "64 Frequently Asked Questions About Asthma and Allergies." *Rodale's Allergy Relief,* February 1989, pp. 1–8.

Woods, Patricia Mason. "Every Breath You Take." *Essence,* June 1992, pp. 28–30, 125–126.

Pamphlets

Alpert, Linda. *Asthma: Fact & Fiction.* Asthma Foundation of Southern Arizona, 1982.

Childhood Asthma: A Matter of Control. American Lung Association, 1990.

Understanding Asthma. National Jewish Center for Immunology and Respiratory Medicine, 1992.

What You Need to Know About Asthma. National Institute of Allergy and Infectious Diseases, March 1990.

Your Asthma Can Be Controlled: Expect Nothing Less. Public Health Service, National Institutes of Health, 1991.

Your Child and Asthma. National Jewish Center for Immunology and Respiratory Medicine, 1992.

Internet Resources

gopher://fido.nhlbi.nih.gov:70/00/educprog/naepp/ (National Asthma Education and Prevention Program)

http://galen.med.virginia.edu/- smb4v/tutorials/asthma/asthma1.html (an asthma tutorial for children with sound clips and short movies)

http://pathfinder.com/@@jSkgzDKtawAAQCaf/HLC/lookitup/condit ions/ asth.html (The Healthy Living Channel: Asthma)

http://www.asthma.com/what.html (Asthma Zero Mortality Coalition)

http://www.cco.caltech.edu/-wrean/asthma-gen.html (alt.support.asthma FAQ: Asthma—General Information)

http://www.execpc.com/-edi/aaaai.html (American Academy of Allergy Asthma & Immunology Information and resources)

http://www.njc.org/ (National Jewish Center for Immunology and Respiratory Medicine home page with many links to information)

http://www.podi.com/health/aanma/aandesc.html (Allergy and Asthma Network/Mothers of Asthmatics)

Index

heredity, 14, 25, 26, 109
Hippocrates, 12, 112
histamine, 20, 40, 52, 71
histamine-releasing
     factor (HRF), 106
holistic approach, 77
homeopathy, 77
house dust, 5, 9, 20, 25,
     81, 82
Hurst, Allan, 18, 113
hyperreactive airways, 5,
     8, 11, 20, 25, 28,
     35, 42, 68, 113

I

immune system, 37-38
immunoglobulin E
     (IgE), 19, 38, 40,
     42, 54, 75, 105,
     106, 113
immunoglobulin G
     (IgG), 38, 75
immunotherapy, 5, 74-75
incidence of asthma, 24-
     25
inflammation, 5, 8, 9,
     20, 22, 28, 31, 40,
     45, 52, 60, 66, 68,
     72, 79, 113
inhalers, 5, 45, 64-65, 99
intracutaneous test, 54
Ishizaka, Kimishige and
     Teruko, 19, 113
isoprenaline
     (isoproterenol), 74
Itkin, Irving, 20, 113

J

Joyner-Kersee, Jackie,
     21-22, 37

K

Katz, Roger, 22

L

larynx, 26, 48
late-phase response, 31
leukotrienes, 108
lung function in asthma,
     28, 30, 43

lung volume
     measurements, 51

M

magnesium, 78
ma huang, 73, 112
Maimonides, 14, 112
marijuana, 110
Masone, Elysa, 92
mast cells, 40, 54, 71, 105
methacholine, 52
molds, 5, 9, 20, 32, 82,
     84, 110
mucus, 9, 12, 30, 35, 40,
     42, 62, 63, 69, 89

N

National Home for
     Jewish Children, 17
nedocromil, 71
nighttime (nocturnal)
     asthma, 42-43, 49,
     56, 60, 61, 72
nitrogen dioxide, 98

O

Olympics, 22, 35, 37, 39
ozone, 85, 98, 101

P

parentectomy, 18, 19, 112
peak flow, 60, 61
peak flow meter, 56, 58, 63
perfume, 85, 87
Peshkin, C. Murray, 17-
     18, 19, 112
pets, 32, 84
pharynx, 26
Pliny the Elder, 73
pollen, 5, 9, 20, 25, 32,
     40, 80, 87, 89
prevention, 80-91
prick test, 54
Primatene Mist, 44, 45, 99
pulmonary function
     tests, 51-54
purse-lip breathing, 90

R

radioallergosorbent test
     (RAST), 54, 56

ragweed, 32, 40, 87
Roosevelt, Theodore, 7-8

S

secondhand smoke, 34,
     92-93, 95-96
self management, 63-64
shortness of breath, 5,
     30, 44, 45
skin testing, 54
Sorvino, Paul, 75-76
spacer, 64, 65
spirometry, 51, 52
sputum analysis, 50
stages of severity, 60-61,
     65-66
steroids, 66, 69-71, 72,
     74
stress, 9, 20, 35
summer camps, 103-104
support groups, 103
symptoms, 5, 30-31, 45,
     47, 58, 60-61

T

Taylor, Krissy, 44-45
terbutaline, 39
theophylline, 16, 39, 69,
     72
tightness in the chest, 5,
     8
Torre, Arthur, 60, 61, 66
trachea, 26
treatment, 5, 62-79, 110
triggers, 5, 20, 32-35,
     52, 66, 81, 84, 85,
     89, 113
twitchy lungs, 20, 25

V

vagus nerve, 68
ventilation
     measurement, 52
vital capacity (VC), 51
vocal cord dysfunction
     (VCD), 48

W

wheal, 54
wheezing, 5, 8, 30, 45,
     48, 78, 109, 112

128